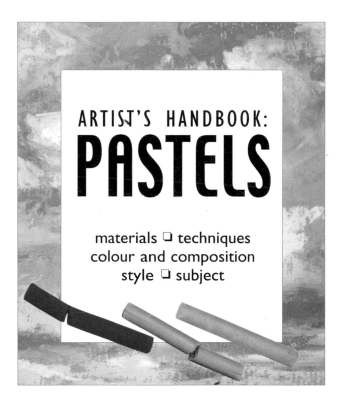

ARTIST'S HANDBOOK:
PASTELS

materials ❏ techniques
colour and composition
style ❏ subject

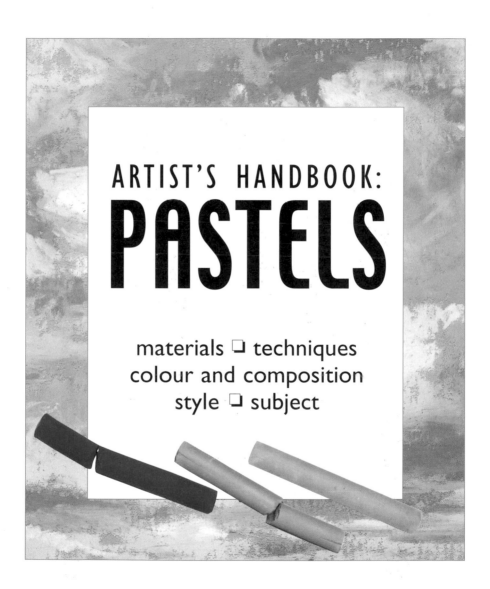

ARTIST'S HANDBOOK:
PASTELS

materials ❏ techniques
colour and composition
style ❏ subject

angus

AN OCEANA BOOK

This book is produced by
Oceana Books
6 Blundell Street
London
N7 9BH

This edition printed 2004
Published by Angus Books Ltd.
12 Ravensbury Terrace
London
SW18 4RL

ISBN 1-904594-20-4

QUMPAH3

Manufactured in Singapore by
Pica Digital Pte Ltd
Printed in Hong Kong by
Paramount Printing Co. Ltd

CONTENTS

INTRODUCTION

There must be few artists who have not
wanted to try their hand at painting with
pastels at some time or other. Perhaps the
reason for this is the beauty of the pastels
themselves. Unlike paints, which hide their
colours in metal tubes, pastels are not shy
about displaying their charms.

Pastel is an immensely satisfying medium, and
in many ways ideal for beginners. A child
takes its early steps in art with chalk or
crayons rather than paints and brushes,
relishing the ease of spreading colour on paper.
And so it is for the inexperienced artist. With
any of the other painting media, you must
premix your colours on a palette, learn how to
handle brushes, and spend time drawing before
you can apply colour. Pastels needs none of
these intermediary stages, because it is both a
drawing and a painting medium. The stick of
colour becomes virtually an extension of your
hand: Just as the child does, you can simply
pick it up and start painting.

The Pleasure of Pastels

Because pastel is such a rapid and responsive medium, it is ideal for recording the fleeting, transitory effects so often found in nature. Melting mists, scudding clouds, crushing waves – all these can be captured with a few rapid, decisive strokes. There are no colours to be premixed, no drying times to worry about, no brushes to be kept clean – in short, no tiresome procedures to dampen your enthusiasm or dull your response to the subject.

The unique quality of pastels is their versatility; they can be used as both a drawing and a painting medium. Simply by twisting and turning the crayon, using the tip and then the side, you can create several different effects – fine, precise lines; broad, sweeping strokes and solid, dense layers of colour – and these can be combined in an almost infinite number of ways. Thus pastel is equally appropriate for highly finished, complex studies and for rapid impressions.

The colours are not only immensely varied, from soft, delicate tints to bright, vibrant hues and rich, deep darks, but also extremely pure and luminous, due in part to the way

LAVENDER FIELDS by Lionel Aggett

in which light reflects off the myriad particles on the surface of the painting. Furthermore, pastel colours remain fresh and lively from the start, and do not change colour when applied, unlike watercolour, for example, which appears much paler when dry, or oil paint, which sinks into the canvas and can darken or even crack with age.

On the purely practical level, pastels are simple and convenient to use. You don't need much in the way of extra equipment such as brushes, knives and mixing mediums, and no preparation of the painting surface is necessary. Just lay out your pastels and you're ready to start. When you're finished, all you need to do is put away your pastels – there are no brushes to clean, no palette to scrape, and no need to cover up the pigments to stop them from drying out.

Of course, pastel does have its drawbacks, too – but what medium doesn't? One of the great masters of pastel painting, Quentin de la Tour (1704–1788), once wrote to a friend: 'Pastels, my Lord Marquis, involve a number of further obstacles such as dust, the weakness of some pigments, the fact that the tone is never correct, and that one must blend one's colours on the paper itself and apply a number of strokes with different crayons instead of one, that there is a risk of spoiling the work done, and

that one has no expedient if its spir is lost.' So if you do encounter difficulties with the medium, take heart – you are in good company!

The most obvious drawback of pastel is its fragility. The sticks sometimes crumble and break under pressure, and a pastel painting is vulnerable to accidental smudging and smearing if it is not mounted under glass or protected with fixative.

Also, though pastels are easier to handle and more immediate in use than oil paints are, they are less flexible. For example, you can't mix pigments on the palette to achieve just the right colour or tone; you must work with a pre-existing range of tints, creating special colour effects directly on the paper. Similarly, mistakes are easily rectified in oils – and to some extent acrylics – by wiping out with a rag or simply overpainting the offending area, but in pastel they require more careful treatment because the surface can easily become clogged, smeared or damaged.

Finally, because pastel is both a drawing and a painting medium, the ability of the artist to draw confidently and well is more important than in some other media. Weak drawing can, to a certain extent, be masked in oil painting; but in pastel the marks made by the artist's hand remain visible and unchanging, so you have to get them right the first time.

A Brief History

Pastels as we know them today – sticks of soft, crumbly colour – have a relatively short history. You may have a vain search in an art gallery to find examples of an 'old master' pastel.

The idea of producing a dry painting medium by binding pigment with gum is credited to an artist named Jean Perréal, who is almost unknown today but had a considerable reputation in his lifetime. Perréal accompanied the French king Louis XII on his Italian campaigns of 1502 and 1509. While in Italy, he met Leonardo da Vinci, who was much impressed by the new colouring method and mentioned Perréal in his notebooks. Leonardo did not use pastel as a full-colour painting medium as we do today, but as a means of adding colour accents to charcoal or red-chalk drawings.

Pastel continued to be used through the 16th and 17th centuries, mainly for portrait sketches, where the flesh tones were often enhanced by the use of a blue paper as background. But it was not until the 18th century that it became accepted as a medium to rival oil paint. This is almost entirely due to a Venetian artist, Rosalba Carriera (1675–1757), whose pastel portraits achieved such success that she quickly became in demand throughout Europe. In 1720 she visited Paris, where her influence was huge. Among the artists to whom she introduced the medium was

CARDINAL MELCHIOR DE POLIGNAC by Rosalba Carriera (*c.* 1732)

Maurice-Quentin de la Tour, who subsequently became the most sought-after artist of his day, and who painted many of his famous contemporaries in pastel, including Madame de Pompadour. He was an exceptional portrait painter who exploited the medium to the full, pioneering a technique of broad strokes that enabled him to work on a large scale – earlier pastel portraits had been quite small.

Another important figure in 18th-century pastel painting was the Swiss miniature painter Jean Etienne Liotard, who did not restrict himself to portraiture but included ambitious figure groups, genre scenes, and still lifes in his pastel repertoire.

CHANGING STYLES AND SUBJECTS

With the exception of Liotard, the use of pastel was confined almost entirely to portraits, in which the notable characteristics are soft blends of colour and a high degree of finish, in line with the then-fashionable style in oil painting. It was not until Edgar Degas began to work in pastels that we see the emergence of a modern style, in which the individual marks of the pastel sticks are encouraged to show rather than being rubbed together and blended.

Many artists tried their hands at pastels in the 19th century, including Eugène Delacroix, the landscape painter Eugène Boudin and Edouard Manet, but Degas is by far the most important in the history of the medium. Always a technical innovator,

he experimented with ways of mixing the pastel with fluid mediums and using various home-made fixatives to set the colours so that he could build up in successive layers. He also pioneered the mixed-media approaches now common, often using pastel colours over his ink monoprints.

Degas saw himself as a draughts-man above all else, and he used pastel in a way that combined drawing and painting. This had not been done before; the 18th-century artists used the medium more or less as a substitute for paint, taking care to obliterate the drawing, or mark-making, element, which they regarded as a weakness in technique.

ELENA CARAFA by Edgar Degas
Degas was one of the great innovators and promoters of pastels. He experimented widely with different techniques, and developed a painting method which involved spraying the pastel surface with warm water or milk.

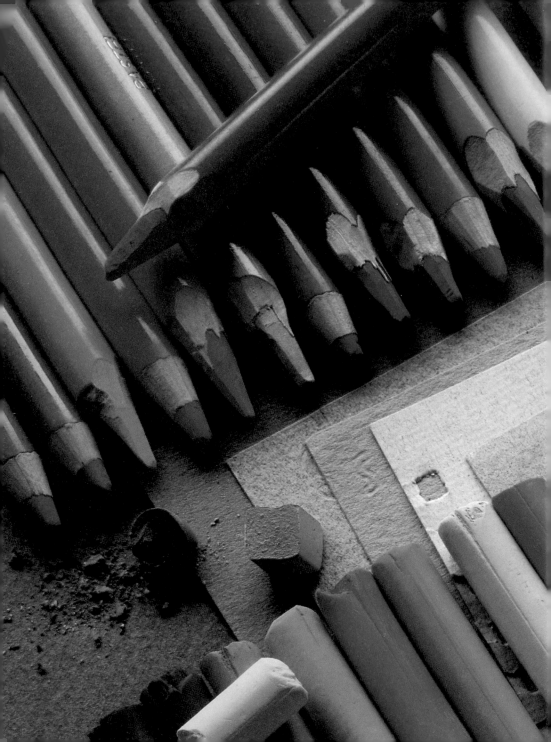

MATERIALS

One of the greatest advantages of pastel painting is that you don't need a great deal in the way of extra equipment – no mixing mediums, brushes, palette knives or unwieldy canvases – just the pastels themselves and a selection of papers. However, you will need to have some idea of which colours to buy, as good pastels are not cheap, and you will need a much wider range than you would for paints. You will also need to know which pastels – hard ones or soft ones – can give the particular effects you're after, and which surfaces to choose – the colour and texture of the paper can be a very important part of a pastel painting.

All About Pastels

Pastels are made from finely ground pigments bound together with a small quantity of gum to form a stiff paste, which is then shaped into round or square sticks and allowed to harden. The word 'pastel', in fact, is derived from the Italian word pastello, *which means paste.*

There are four types of pastel available – soft and hard pastels, pastel pencils and oil pastels. The softness or hardness of a stick is determined by the amount of binder used, the hardness of the pigment, and the degree of pressure applied during the shaping of the sticks. Soft pastels contain just enough binder to keep them in stick form and are combined with white chalk, clay or gypsum to increase their covering power. It is this white filler that is responsible for the delicacy of hue associated with soft pastels, particularly noticeable in the flesh tints. Hard pastels contain more of the gum binder, which makes them stronger; and they're mixed with black pigment instead of chalk, which is why they tend to comprise the darker colours available.

SOFT PASTELS

Soft pastels are the most widely used of the various pastel types because they produce the wonderful velvety bloom that is so typical of the medium. The reason for this is that soft pastels contain very little binder or hardening agent but proportionately more pigment. When you use them, you'll notice how rich and vibrant their colours are and how smoothly the pastel stick glides across the surface of the paper.

The loose, grainy texture of soft pastels provides great colour clarity, but it is also the reason why many people find pastels difficult to use. The powdery colour can seem to spread uncontrollably, and it is aggravating when a fragile pastel stick snaps or crumbles in the middle of a stroke. This can lead to a cautious approach, but the best results come from working freely and decisively.

Since the degree of softness varies noticeably from one brand of pastel to another, try out individual sticks from different manufacturers until you find the one that suits you best.

HARD PASTELS

Hard pastels have a greater proportion of binder to pigment, so they are more stable in use than soft pastels, but they do not have such wide potential for varied surface effects. Traditionally, they are used for preliminary sketching of a composition, and for adding linear detail and sharpening touches to soft pastel work. In effect, hard pastels are the drawing medium that complements soft pastels as a painting medium. You can exploit the linear qualities by using the section edge of the stick, or even sharpening it to a point by shaving it with a fine blade. There are also several techniques you can use to develop effects of massed colour, such as shading, hatching and crosshatching (see Techniques). The colour range is quite limited by comparison with soft pastels, with nothing like the degrees of variation in hue and tone.

PASTEL PENCILS

Pastel pencils are thin pastel sticks encased in wood, just like normal pencils. They are more expensive to buy, but it is a good idea to always have a few on hand because they are ideal for subjects that entail intricate work. Pastel pencils can be sharpened to a point, using sandpaper or a craft knife, to produce extremely fine, crisp lines. Because of their length and resistance to snapping or crumbling, pastel pencils give you greater control of handling and are excellent for techniques such as crosshatching and feathering. Another advantage, of course, is that your fingers stay clean!

OIL PASTELS

This medium is unique among the pastel types, containing an oil binder that makes the texture dense and greasy and the colours slightly less opaque than soft pastels. Typically, the colours are quite strong and the variation of colour values is restricted. The moist texture of oil pastel can quickly fill the grain of the paper, so the capacity to work one colour over another is somewhat limited, but for painting effects, oil pastel marks can be softened and spread by brushing them with turpentine or white spirit.

WATER-SOLUBLE PASTELS

The wax content of these colour sticks gives them a slightly moist texture, so they handle rather like oil pastels when you use them for drawn strokes. But brush over the colour with clean water and it instantly dissolves into an even, semi-transparent wash. The quality of the wet colour is like a coarse watercolour wash, and you can vary it considerably according to the amount of water that you add. The restricted colour range is composed of strong, unsubtle hues, but with the potential fluidity of the medium you have more scope for mixing and blending colours on the working surface.

Choosing Your Colours

The main differences between pastels and paints is that you cannot premix colours – any mixing has to be done by laying one colour over another on the painting surface.

To compensate for this limitation, manufacturers produce large ranges of colours and tints, that is, light and dark versions of the same colour. Tints are made by adding white to the pure pigment for the pale tones and black for the dark ones.

The colours are given names that usually, but not always, correspond to the pigment name. Certain pigments cannot be used for pastels because they may pose a health risk, so you may find a red labelled 'bright red' rather than vermilion or cadmium red. The tints are usually denoted by a number, from 1 to 6 or more. Manufacturers' numbering systems vary, but in most cases the lower numbers are paler tints, with the darker tints at the top of the scale and the pure colour in the middle.

Because there are such a bewildering array of colours, how do you choose a manageable quantity to suit your needs? One way is to start by thinking about what sort of subject you like to paint and choose your palette of colours accordingly. If your subject is landscapes, obviously you'll need a lot of greens and earth colours. For portraits, you'll need a range of flesh tones plus a few extra colours for the sitter's clothing; and if you are a flower painter, you can really go to town with bright, vibrant colours. Even so, you will always need a selection of neutral colours for the shadows and highlights, such as a range of greys and beiges.

Another way to go is to start out with one of the boxed sets of pastels that manufacturers produce. These come in many sizes, from a simple set of 12 colours to a deluxe set of 300, and you can even buy pre-selected assortments specially for the landscape or portrait painter.

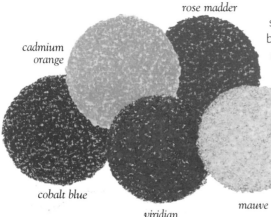

rose madder

cadmium orange

cobalt blue

viridian

mauve

A Recommended Starter Palette

Many beginning artists start with one of the small boxed sets (usually containing 12 sticks of pastels) produced especially for newcomers to the medium. If it does not include black, for example, or has only one red, you may need to buy these colours separately.

The 26 colours shown here provide a range of values suitable for most subjects. Of course, you can add more as you need them.

Ultramarine blue No. 6

Ultramarine blue No. 1

Prussian blue No. 3

Cerulean blue No. 4

Purple No. 6

Mauve No. 2

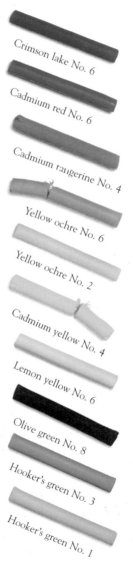

Crimson lake No. 6

Cadmium red No. 6

Cadmium tangerine No. 4

Yellow ochre No. 6

Yellow ochre No. 2

Cadmium yellow No. 4

Lemon yellow No. 6

Olive green No. 8

Hooker's green No. 3

Hooker's green No. 1

Sap green No. 5

Lizard green No. 3

Green-grey No. 1

Blue-grey No. 4

Cool grey No. 4

Burnt umber No. 8

Raw umber No. 6

Burnt sienna No. 4

Silver white

Lamp black

Taking Care of Your Pastels

A boxed set of pastels contains a tray of preformed slots to which you can return your sticks after each working session. But if you choose a starter palette of loose pastels, it makes sense to consider ways of organizing the pastels neatly and keeping them separated so that they remain clean.

You can buy special boxes for loose pastels but these are expensive. You can save money by using your ingenuity. For example, corrugated cardboard is ideal for separating pastels, and you can use it to line the small oblong cardboard boxes in which manufacturers package their pastels and tubes of paint.

As you build up your collection of sticks, you will need a larger container, so keep your eyes open for a long, flat box with a well-fitting lid. If you have no corrugated cardboard, you could line the box with ground rice. This not only cushions the pastels but also helps to keep them clean, because the rice absorbs the dust that always collects on the surface of the sticks.

CLEANING PASTELS

However carefully you store your pastels, you cannot always keep them clean when you are working. Eventually, they will become dirty, because pastel dust on your hands will be transferred to a previously clean stick. They can be cleaned easily with ground rice or a similar grain, such as semolina.

1 *Put your dirty pastels into a container full of ground rice and shake them gently until all the muddy-coloured dust has been absorbed by the grain.*

2 *Empty the contents of the container into a sieve or a colander to strain off the rice. Your pastels are now clean.*

Surfaces for Pastel Work

Because pastel is such a soft, crumbly medium, it does not adhere well to a smooth surface. Because of this, pastel papers are manufactured with a slight 'tooth', or texture, which 'bites' the powdery pigment and holds it in place.

There are several types of paper made especially for pastel work. The two best-known and most readily available are Ingres paper and Canson Mi-Teintes. The first has a pattern of straight lines, while the texture of the second resembles fine chicken wire. But Mi-Teintes is effectively two papers in one, as you can use the smoother side if you prefer – it has a less obtrusive texture but it still holds the pastel.

If you like to work thickly, you may want to experiment with three other kinds of paper: sandpaper, pastel board and velour paper. Sandpaper, made for carpentry work and available in different grades from very coarse to very fine, is popular with pastel painters – usually the finer ones are chosen. Some art suppliers produce a version specifically for

pastels, called artists' sandpaper, which comes in much larger sheets. Buying pastel board can be confusing, because it is also known under a variety of brand names, including Sansfix paper and Bristol board, but most pastel board is made from tiny particles of cork pressed together to give a surface a little like sandpaper but less scratchy. Some pastel board is made by laminating two sheets of watercolour paper together, which gives a much smoother surface. Velour paper has a lovely velvety feel, and gives a soft line.

You can also work on papers not specifically designed for pastel work, such as watercolour paper, a popular choice among many pastel painters. This paper has a relatively heavy texture that holds the pigment well, but because it is white, you may want to colour it. As you will see on page 21, pastel papers are nearly always coloured.

A selection of Mi-Teintes and Fabriano Ingres papers in various colours.

Paper Colour

Pastels can be done on white paper, but this is the exception. Coloured papers are usually chosen, and paper manufacturers produce a large range, from neutral greys and beiges to vivid primary hues.

The reason for working on coloured papers is simple and practical. As we have seen, pastel papers have a surface texture, so unless the colour is applied very heavily, it is virtually impossible to cover the paper completely. The colour sits on top of the raised texture, and there are always flecks and patches of naked paper showing between and around the strokes. If the paper is white, this creates a disturbing, jumpy effect in the finished picture.

Moreover, it is difficult to work on a white surface because it is hard to assess the first colours you put on. Since everything looks dark against white, you may find that you begin with colours that are much too pale, setting a wrong colour key for the picture. A grey or beige paper allows you to judge both the light and the dark colours because it provides a middle tone.

Pastel is a partnership between pigment and paper, and if the colour of the paper is chosen with care, it enhances the work. In many pictures, large areas of paper are deliberately left uncovered. Landscapes are often done on blue or blue-grey paper, with the sky left as the paper colour. In portraits the face and figure may be worked in pastel, while the background consists entirely or almost entirely of the paper colour, perhaps with a few light strokes to suggest furniture or a window frame to give a context to the figure.

Additional Equipment

One of the many attractions of pastel work is that you do not need much equipment; the basic requirements are pastels and paper. However, there are a few additional items that you may find useful.

BULLDOG CLIPS

Bulldog clips can be used for holding paper on a thin drawing board, such as plywood or hardboard.

CRAFT KNIFE

A craft knife is useful for sharpening pastel pencils and for cutting paper.

KNEADED ERASER

These are useful because they can be pinched into a small point for erasing small areas. (A small piece of kneaded white bread also works well.)

BRUSHES

Brushes are not essential, but are useful for blending and for flicking off excess pastel.

FIXATIVE

Fixative comes in aerosol spray cans or spray-pump bottles.

TORCHONS

Torchons are narrow tubes of rolled blotting paper used for blending colours. You can use your fingertip just as easily, but torchones (also called tortillons) are rigid and pointed at the tip, making them good for small, detailed areas. They also minimize the risk of grease from your skin spoiling the painting.

COTTON BUDS

Cotton buds are an inexpensive alternative to torchons.

COTTON WOOL

Cotton wool is good for large scale blending.

PROTECTING THE FLOOR

Even an uncarpeted floor needs protection while you work, because pastel dust flies around if you try to sweep it up. Put an old sheet or plastic dustsheet under your easel. Shake it outside gently when you have finished working.

RAGS

Rags or kitchen paper for cleaning your hands periodically are essential – pastel is a messy medium. Rags are also useful for blending.

MASKING TAPE

For fastening large sheets of paper to the drawing board, masking tape is better than bulldog clips.

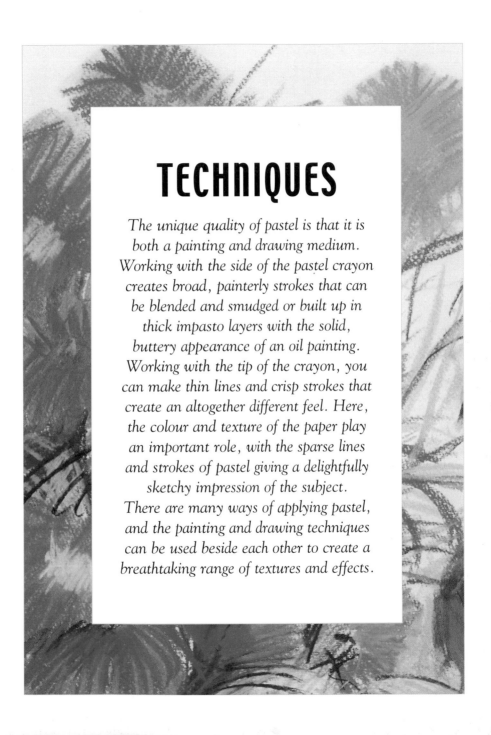

TECHNIQUES

The unique quality of pastel is that it is both a painting and drawing medium. Working with the side of the pastel crayon creates broad, painterly strokes that can be blended and smudged or built up in thick impasto layers with the solid, buttery appearance of an oil painting. Working with the tip of the crayon, you can make thin lines and crisp strokes that create an altogether different feel. Here, the colour and texture of the paper play an important role, with the sparse lines and strokes of pastel giving a delightfully sketchy impression of the subject. There are many ways of applying pastel, and the painting and drawing techniques can be used beside each other to create a breathtaking range of textures and effects.

BASIC TECHNIQUES
Line Strokes

The marks you make with your sticks of colour are the bricks and mortar of your pastel paintings. They can describe form and volume, convey texture and create outline and detail. And, more than this, they are your personal handwriting, making your work different from that of any other artist.

The more you can practise, the better. You will gain experience in handling pastels as well as build up a repertoire of marks. After a while you will know instinctively which ones to use in your paintings, just as the process of handwriting becomes so automatic that you no longer consider how each letter and word are formed.

The strokes made with the tip or edge of the pastel stick can be infinitely varied, so begin by doodling to see how many different ones you can achieve. Try long, light strokes; short, jabbing ones; curves and dots. Try making strokes that change from light to heavy, or from fine to thick, depending upon the pressure you apply and the angle of the pastel stick to the paper.

Experiment with ways of holding the pastel. For light strokes you can guide it loosely with your fingers near the top end. For short, dense marks requiring greater pressure, you will need to grip the stick near the drawing end. If pastels break, as they will under pressure, do not worry, because you will need smaller lengths to try out the side strokes described on pages 28–29.

HEAVY PRESSURE
Heavy pressure, with the pastel pushed into the paper grain, gives stronger colour.

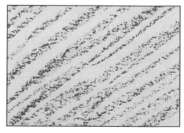

LIGHT PRESSURE
The lighter the pressure, the paler the colour will look, as the pastel only partially covers the paper.

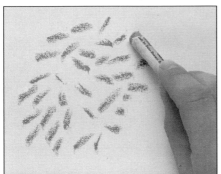

🖋 Make short, straight, jabbing strokes, holding the pastel near the end.

🖙 Try several colours, making strokes that follow different directions and overlap one another.

🖙 Try a range of squiggly marks made with a blunted point.

🖙 Vary the stroke from thin to thick, starting with a sharp edge which becomes progressively worn down.

🖙 Make short strokes with the sharp tip of the pastel.

🖙 Use the edge of the stick to draw fine lines and long, sweeping strokes.

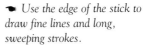

Side Strokes

Line strokes give excitement to a pastel painting because they are immediately noticeable, but side strokes can be equally expressive in a quieter way. Although these are the strokes to choose for covering large areas, that is not their only application.

Side strokes can be nearly as varied as line strokes, depending upon the pressure, the direction of the stroke and the size of the piece of pastel used. This last point is important, because to make side strokes you have to sacrifice some of your sticks of colour and break them into pieces of a suitable length to create the effect you want.

Take a piece of pastel 1 to 5 cm ($\frac{1}{2}$ to 2 in) long, and rub it over the paper to create a flat side. Then try different directions of strokes – from long, straight, even ones to short curves – and different pressures. You will see that a heavy pressure forces the pigment into the grain of the paper, while light pressure creates a veil of colour on the surface. Pressure can be varied in a single stroke, creating a gradation from light to dark.

Side strokes are useful for covering large areas. They are also one of the most expressive of all the pastel strokes, and many different effects can be created by varying the pressure of the pastel on the paper. Smooth papers are best for detailed work or fine lines; but because they have little tooth to hold the pastel particles, they quickly become clogged if too many layers are worked on top of one another.

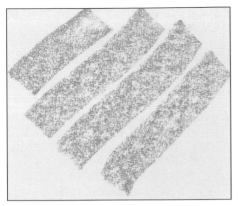

● *Make broad strokes with a 2.5 cm (1 in) length of pastel and medium pressure.*

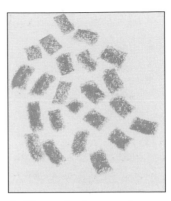

● *Then make shorter strokes with a 1 cm (¹/₂ in) piece and heavier pressure.*

● *Make long strokes, varying the pressure from heavy to light and twisting the stick slightly.*

● *Angle the pastel stick in different ways so that the marks change from thick to thin.*

➤ *Try a series of curves, following different directions, and again varying the pressure.*

When side strokes are used on rough paper, the grainy effect produced can be used to suggest specific textures, such as tree bark, woven fabric, or perhaps a pebbly beach. However, bear in mind that this technique works best when used wisely and as a contrast to linear work.

Blending

The powdery texture of pastel, which is one of the properties that can make pastel hard to handle, can also be turned to your advantage. If you have ever rested your hand on a work in progress, you are familiar with how easily crisp lines can become smudged. Accidentally, you have discovered a primary technique of working in pastel – blending.

Blending simply means rubbing one colour into another and into the paper so that any lines are softened, and colours and tones merge with no perceptible boundaries. The technique is excellent for creating diffused effects – misty skies, for example – and for any areas of a painting that are intended to recede, such as the background of a portrait or still life.

For large areas, such as skies, it is best to lay on the colour with the broad side of the pastel stick and then to blend with a rag, kitchen paper, large brush, or the flat of your hand. The last way is often preferable, since both rags and brushes remove a good deal of colour – making a lot of dust in the process – whereas the small amount of oil in your skin mixes with the pastel and makes it adhere to the paper, so that it is more easily pushed into the paper's surface.

Blending can also be a remedial measure. If you are building an image mainly with linear strokes and find that in one area the marks look too harsh or the colours too bright, simply rub gently over them for a softened effect.

Because it is so easy to create soft effects and mixed colours by blending, the method tends to be overused by beginners, and this can result in a bland picture. If you find this happening, use your blended areas as a base, spray the piece with fixative, and work over it with more energetic strokes, using soft or hard pastels.

HAND BLENDING

1 *For a windswept sky, place several bands of light and dark colour one above the other. Then soften the boundaries between colours with the side of your hand.*

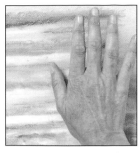

2 *You can alter colours or introduce others as you progress. Add brown to suggest the warmer hues of sunset. Apply it lightly with the point of the pastel or the side of a short stick.*

3 *Use your finger or thumb to rub the colours into one another and blend the edges of the strokes.*

4 *Hand blending is particularly effective, because it creates less dust than merging the pastel with brushes.*

BLENDING WITH A PAINTBRUSH

1 *A paintbrush is good for conveying a diffused effect over an extensive area. Use broad side strokes and brush along, not across, them to blend.*

2 *Beginning with broad, light strokes is the key to successful blending. The brush will remove a good deal of the colour, leaving the strokes blurred but still visible.*

3 *Foreground areas need to be more definite, so use point strokes for the grasses and brush gently over them to soften the edges.*

31

MIXED BLENDING METHODS

The rich colours of this sky were achieved by applying one colour over another and blending them with sweeping motions of the hand. Smaller areas were blended with the fingertips, and for the grasses shown in the detail, the artist used hard pastels over a layer of yellow-brown, blending them with a torchon (see page 33).

BLENDING SMALL AREAS

The loose blending described on the previous pages is fine for skies and backgrounds, but not as suitable when it comes to small areas that you need to control precisely. If you are painting a still life or flower and want a gentle gradation of colour and tone to build up form, perhaps on petals or on the curve of a vase, blend with a finger or a torchon.

A torchon, or rolled paper stump, is perfect for small areas such as eyes, lips, or flower stems but must be used with caution, since a new torchon has a sharp point and can dig into the paper and damage it. Cotton buds are tailor-made for working in small areas. The firm swabs of cotton, with their rounded ends, give excellent control and do not damage the paper, in addition to being inexpensive and readily available.

MAKING AND USING A TORCHON

A torchon, or stump, is a tight roll of paper. You can easily make your own. Begin by cutting a piece of light paper, such as drawing or typing paper, into a tall triangle or a triangle with its top cut off. Turn over the bottom edge and roll up the paper as tightly as possible. Seal the loose end with a touch of glue or a piece of tape. Torchons can also be made from kitchen paper, but you will need a stiffener – try rolling the paper around a cocktail stick.

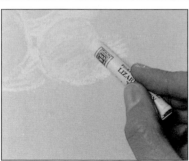

1 *Choose the two shades that most closely match the overall colour of the fruit, and apply them lightly.*

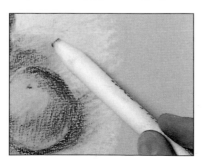

2 *Begin building up the forms with darker colours, using the torchon to blend the shadow areas only.*

3 *To avoid overblending, decide where subtle effects are most important. The edge of the shadow needs softening, so use the torchon here, and also for the halo of reflected light at the bottom of each piece of fruit.*

33

Broken Colour

Pastel is an ideal medium for achieving broken-colour effects. The shape and size of the pastel stick and the small-scale gestures your hand makes when manipulating it provide the basic elements of this technique.

Broken colour is a term used to describe an uneven layer of colour that is laid on deliberately so that it only partially covers the surface and allows colours beneath to show through. A sky, for example, might be built up with short, light side strokes of various blues and mauves laid over one another but left unblended, giving a much more vibrant colour effect than flat, blended colour. Line strokes can also be used to create broken-colour effects, with a network of different colours laid over one another, either in a controlled way by hatching and crosshatching, or more randomly.

The aim is to create a coherent but lively area of colour that reads as one colour when viewed from a

PURPLE FIELDS NEAR CENTALDO by Patrick Cullen
In this landscape, each area is interpreted as a complex mass of broken colour, consisting of interwoven and overlaid marks. Careful integration of the colour values gives a coherent structure to the overall view and its individual elements.

distance. This method is sometimes called optical mixing because the colours mix in the eye. The colours must be close in tone, as a juxtaposition of lights and darks will be jumpy and incoherent.

TEATIME, BROWN'S HOTEL by Diana Armfield

In this interior view, the broken-colour effects create a shimmering, atmospheric impression. The colour combinations describe form, texture and pattern, with grainy marks also allowing the tone of the paper to show through in places.

BARGE, THE RAYBELL by Geoff Marsters

In this picture, the pastel strokes are used more emphatically to construct the varied shapes and surface values. The vibrant colour combinations are boldly stated, but carefully arranged to develop the impression of form and space.

Feathering

The term 'feathering' accurately represents the technique – quick, light, linear strokes made with the tip of the pastel, keeping the direction of the strokes consistent.

Feathering couldn't be simpler. All it involves is making light, feathery, diagonal strokes of one colour over another, so that the underlying colour still shows through but is modified by the feathered strokes. For example, if a certain red looks too hot, you can tone it down by feathering over it with strokes of its complementary colour, green. If you've painted an area grey and it looks dull and flat, liven it up with feathered strokes of yellow or red.

This technique works best with a hard pastel or pastel pencil. Soft pastel may smudge and cover the layer below too much. Don't press too hard – use a light, feathery touch to float the colour on top of the existing one.

Feathering is an excellent method for giving new life to colours that have become dull through overblending – something that can easily happen in pastel work. If you have done too much blending, there will be a good deal of pigment on the paper; so spray it with fixative first and then lay some feathered strokes on top in a colour that is slightly more vivid than the blended one. The painting will immediately begin to sparkle.

IHI AT ALDEBURGH by Geoff Marsters
Feathering is used very effectively here to enhance the atmospheric qualities of the image and create subtly vibrant colour mixes.

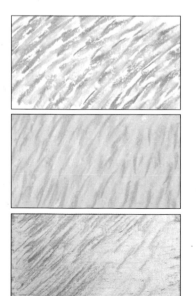

This area of blended hues is built up on the white ground of the paper by overlaying light, quick strokes of pink, purple and pale blue.

The same colours are used here on a flat ground of yellow pastel. Each successive colour application modifies the effect of individual hues.

Very fine, elongated strokes are used here to produce a shimmering effect of colour and texture composed of light-toned hues.

Crosshatching

Crosshatching is the classic drawing technique in which tones are built up with lines criss-crossing each other in opposite directions.

Simply by varying the density of the strokes, you can create a wide range of tones; closely spaced lines with a dark pastel on a light-toned paper will create a dark tone, and widely spaced lines a light one, whereas for a light pastel used on a dark paper the opposite applies.

By interweaving different colours you can achieve particularly vibrant colour mixtures. Each hue retains its own identity, but blends partially with adjacent colours in the viewer's eye to create a new colour which can be much more interesting than a single area of flat colour. Also, the lines themselves have life and movement,

adding considerably to the surface interest of the painting. For example, when crosshatching is used in a figure painting, it somehow conveys the impression of life more effectively than flat colour does.

Crosshatching, as a linear technique, has an advantage over blending in that dense, glowing colour can be created without prematurely filling up the tooth of the paper, thus retaining a fresh, lively appearance.

Crosshatching works best on a smooth paper and can be used with all types of pastel, separately or in combination. However, hard pastels

There is almost no end to the effects that can be achieved by altering the space and direction of crosshatched strokes. Here diagonal crosshatching has been used on top of vertical and horizontal strokes.

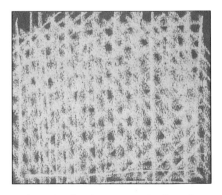

In this example, the same strokes have been used, but in four different colours, which vastly extends the possibilities of the technique.

and pastel pencils are the most suitable for this technique because they give sharper, crisper lines. For even greater textural variety, the crosshatched lines can be softened partially in places by stroking them lightly with your thumb.

Crosshatching is normally done with diagonal strokes running in opposite directions, but you can also build up a denser web of colour by running lines in several different directions – horizontal and vertical, then diagonally in both directions. Practise these techniques, and try different colour mixtures on a variety of toned papers to see what effects you can create.

Altering the pressure used so that some strokes are thicker than others gives even further variety.

Here an interesting pattern has been formed by making several small groups of cross-hatched strokes in different directions.

Traditionally, hatched lines follow the contours of the object. In this simple still life, the lines describe the curved shapes of fruit and bowl, with straight lines emphasizing the flat plane of the tabletop. A limited range of colours is interwoven to create tonal variations giving depth and form.

Scumbling

Like feathering, scumbling is a method of modifying the colour of a toned paper or layer of pastel by applying a thin, opaque layer of another colour over it.

Whereas feathering uses hatched strokes with the point of the pastel, scumbling involves using the side of the stick in a loose motion to create a thin veil of colour which doesn't entirely obliterate the one underneath. The two colours mix optically and have more resonance than an area of flat, blended colour does. The effect is rather like looking at a colour through a thin haze of smoke.

Scumbling creates interesting effects of both colour and texture. Here a light pastel is being used on dark paper.

Scumbling not only creates subtle colour effects, it also gives a very attractive surface texture. Use it to give depth and luminosity to your colours and to soften and unify areas of the painting.

To scumble, use the side of the pastel and make small, circular movements over the area to be covered. Apply only very light pressure, and don't overdo it or the underlay will be completely covered and the effect will be lost. Soft pastel, in particular, requires a very light touch. This technique works best on a paper with plenty of tooth, which won't become clogged too quickly.

1 Scumbling is suitable for large-scale pictures or for backgrounds, where you do not need to control shapes precisely. Scribble lightly over an area of paper, using the side of the pastel stick in a circular motion.

2 After blending the first colour with your fingers, apply a paler layer of scribbled marks in open strokes that will enable the underlying colour to show through.

3 Scumble a pale grey in gentle strokes over the first two colours. Scumbling generally works best with light over dark, but it can be useful for subduing an over-bright colour.

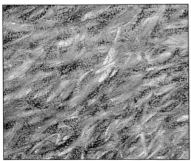

Scumbling light over dark, as here, gives a pleasing shimmer, as the colours are broken up in an irregular way.

THE ARTIST by John Elliot

This portrait has a fascinating ambiguity – the eye is immediately taken by the patriarchal white beard before registering that this is attached to a face not yet aged. In the beard and hair the basic colours are loosely laid in with a form of scumbling, then developed with a complex pattern of brief, vigorous linear marks. In the face, the hatched and shaded colours are more closely integrated, giving the firm profile an imposing, sculptural quality.

Sgraffito

The term sgraffito *derives from the Italian word meaning scratched, and the technique involves working into layered colours with a sharp tool, scratching into the top layer to reveal another colour underneath.*

Sgraffito can, to some extent, be done with soft pastels, but it is much more successful with oil pastels because these adhere more strongly to the paper. It is essential to lay the first colour heavily so that it fills the whole grain of the paper, and the second layer thickly enough to cover the first. For the scratching you need a sharp implement, such as a craft knife.

To achieve a good effect, the colours must be worked out in advance so that you have sufficient colour and tone contrast to make an impact. You might even use the complementary colours, laying red over green, or using a layer of yellow beneath mauve, and scratching into it to create a linear pattern. This could work well in a still life featuring patterned fabrics or ceramic objects. In a landscape, you might begin with yellow overlaid with dark green, and use the method to reveal the yellow in highlighted areas of foliage or grasses.

Another way of using the method is to paint the first colour with acrylic or coloured inks, using oil pastel for the second and any subsequent layers. You are not restricted to two-colour effects.

1 *After making a drawing, the artist lays on the oil pastel thickly, starting with the dark purple, which she intends to scratch into.*

2 *She has added further colours to build up the form, but she relies on the sgraffito to provide the sharp definition, using the point of a knife to make fine lines.*

3 *In this area, several colours have been layered over one another, and the knife is used to scratch away the top layers. The surface is a heavy watercolour paper, thick enough to withstand this treatment.*

OIL PASTEL OVER WATERCOLOUR

1 *The base colour is painted with a loose wash of yellow-green watercolour. When this is dry, black oil pastel is shaded thickly over the surface and rubbed to produce a smoothly blended texture.*

2 *The drawing is begun with the tip of a craft-knife blade, taking care just to scratch back the oil pastel colour and avoid digging into the paper surface.*

3 *This example is worked as a line drawing, using closely hatched lines to produce the impression of variations of colour and tone.*

Sfumato

The characteristic of the effect called sfumato (an Italian word meaning smoke-like) is a soft, hazy quality in which tones and colours merge into each other and build an image without reliance on linear structure or emphasis on edges and contours.

Like several commonly used pastel painting techniques, *sfumato* derives from traditions first established in oil painting. *Sfumato* is not a technique in itself, but a visual quality, and you can achieve the effect by using any of the techniques that enable you to apply controlled, subtle colour transitions: blending, colour gradation, scumbling and shading. If your image has a varied range of tones and a shadowy or atmospheric mood, you can also use careful erasure to lift light out of dark and develop gentle contrasts of light and shade.

To create the picture below, the subject was first blocked in with blue and grey soft pastels on a buff coloured paper, using sketchy outlines and loose hatching to define the areas of light and shade. The pastel strokes were softened and spread with a torchon to make the marks less linear and allow the colours to merge. Then the colour areas were gradually built up in lightly shaded layers. Dark tones were smudged with thumb and fingers to create patches of soft shadow. The form of the cat's head was developed with dark and light tones. The colours were freely applied using the tip and side of the pastel sticks and blended using fingers or a torchon as appropriate. In the final stages, the features were drawn with feathery pastel strokes, some blended into the previous colour and others remaining more clearly defined. Although there are no hard edges or distinct outlines, the dramatic use of light and shade makes a highly descriptive impression of form and contour.

Stippling

Stippling is the technique of using dot patterns to build an impression of shape and form. It is particularly associated with monochrome drawing, a way of modelling forms through tonal gradations of light and shade.

The size and spacing of the dots in stippling is varied so that different areas of the dot pattern convey different tonal densities when viewed from a distance. In colour work, stippling can be used to enliven areas of massed colour, using either individual or closely related hues, or mixed colours applied directly to the support or over a light layer of pastel colour already laid in.

If you stipple with soft pastels or oil pastels, you are likely to achieve quite a coarse, irregular stippling. Even if you sharpen the end of the pastel to begin with, it immediately wears down in use. With hard pastels or pastel pencils you can obtain a finer, more controlled effect because these media do not spread so rapidly. Pencils can be sharpened frequently to maintain a true point, and the corner of a square-sectioned hard pastel will also give you quite a precise, confined mark.

PASTEL PENCIL (*above*)
The harder, fine tips of pastel pencils provide the means for very fine stippling, but this means that covering a large area of the paper may be very time-consuming.

SOFT PASTEL (*left*)
Depending on the pressure you apply to the pastel tip, the effect of stippling in soft pastel can range from fine to very coarse. Integrating dots of different colours enables you to build up an increasingly detailed image, with graded hues and tones modelling individual aspects of the form.

Underdrawing

Because pastel is both a drawing and a painting medium, you do not always need to make a preliminary underdrawing. You can start off in colour and draw as you work.

For any subject involving a variety of shapes that need to be carefully related, such as a still life or figure painting, it is advisable to establish a good foundation. Pastel pencils, hard pastel sticks and charcoal are all suitable for preliminary work.

Charcoal has an advantage over both pastel pencil and hard pastel, which are difficult to erase if the drawing goes wrong. You can brush down any incorrect charcoal lines

with a rag or your hand and draw over them. This way you can be confident of getting the shapes and composition right before you lay on the colour. To avoid sullying the pastel colours, fix the charcoal drawing when you have finished it, or brush it down with a broad brush to remove the excess dust.

If you have an existing drawing or photograph that you want to use as the basis for a pastel, you might like

PASTEL PENCIL

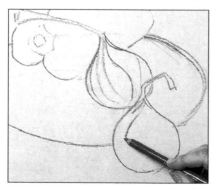

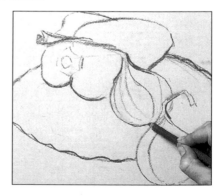

1 *Pastel pencil is less forgiving than charcoal because it is less easy to erase, so do your best to be accurate from the start, and choose a colour that will blend in with those of the subject.*

2 *Concentrate on outline, avoiding shading, and strengthen the lines only in places that will be dark in the painting, such as the bottoms of the fruit and plate here. If you make heavy lines in light-coloured areas, you may not be able to cover them.*

to try a method called pouncing. The original picture is traced, holes are pierced along the traced-in lines, and charcoal or pastel dust (pounce) is applied with a pounce bag through the holes onto the paper. To make the holes, you can use either a perforating wheel or a pointed implement, such as a large needle – the former is quicker. This technique is used for painting murals and by embroiderers for making designs onto fabric.

CHARCOAL

1 *Medium-thickness willow charcoal is best for underdrawing; thinner sticks break easily. Hold the stick loosely near the top end and begin sketching the main lines of the underdrawing.*

2 *Errors can be erased quickly. Rub the charcoal off immediately with your finger before redrawing.*

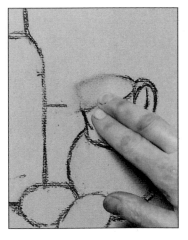

3 *Correct the drawing, erasing again if necessary. The rubbed-down charcoal leaves a grey smear, but this will not affect the pastel colour.*

Underpainting

To begin a pastel painting, it is common practise to block in the main shapes and colours with light side strokes and gradually build up with further layers of colour, but an alternative method is to work over an underpainting, made in acrylic or watercolour.

An underpainting can be monochromatic, in which case it serves the purpose of establishing the tonal structure of the picture, but more often it is in colour, and resembles a light colour sketch.

The advantage of this method is that it allows you to cover the paper quickly, so that you can complete the painting with fewer layers of pastel colour, allowing areas of the underpainting to show through. Some artists use similar colours for the underpainting as for the final work, while others exploit contrasts, painting yellow on an area that is to be blue-grey, or using red under green for a sparkling complementary contrast of colours.

Standard pastel papers are quite thin and will not accept water without buckling. Water will spoil the surface of pastel board or sandpaper, so watercolour paper is the best choice for this method.

1 *If the subject is colourful, it makes sense to give it a ground of bright colour. Working on watercolour paper, use a broad brush to apply strong washes of watercolour (or acrylic).*

2 *Cover the entire surface with paint, applying darker colours where you want to build up dark tones of pastel. The deep purple here will be allowed to show through the lighter pastel colours for shadows.*

3 *Allow the underpainting to dry thoroughly before working with pastel. Then use short side strokes in various colours to create broken-colour effects, suggesting flowers and foliage.*

4 *Continue to build up the picture with small strokes. Do not try to cover the underpainting; the essence of this method is to leave parts of the watercolour showing between and beneath the pastel marks.*

5 *Now use the tip of the pastel to begin refining shapes and introducing small contrasts of colour. Notice how the orange underpainting shows through the blue of the sky to give the painting a lively sparkle.*

6 *Flecks of yellow and orange under-painting enliven the areas of green and enhance the vibrant colour effects. The heavy grain of the paper helps by breaking up the pastel strokes to suggest texture – especially evident on the path.*

Using Thick Colour

In some pastel paintings you can see that the colour is so thickly applied that it almost resembles oil paint. Such works are produced by a variety of overlaying methods – they sometimes involve wet brushing and often call for the use of fixative at various stages.

You can lay colour thickly on Canson Mi-Teintes paper if you build up gradually from initial light applications, but the best surfaces to use for this kind of work are sandpaper, velour paper and pastel board.

Sandpaper is something of an acquired taste. If you want to try the effect without spending much money, buy a small sheet of carpenters' sandpaper (fine grade) and see how you like it.

Smooth watercolour paper is also favoured by some artists who work with thick colour, but because it has little texture to hold the pastel, it will not stand too great a degree of overworking. It is best used, therefore, in conjunction with a watercolour or acrylic underpainting (see pages 50–51), which allows you to restrict yourself to one or two layers of heavily applied pastel.

IMPASTO EFFECTS

Impasto means applying paint so thickly that you can see raised edges. In pastel work, you can achieve an equivalent result by using the full strength and texture of the pigment in heavy strokes. Mounting sandpaper on a rigid surface enabled this artist to apply maximum pressure. The detail shows that, on the branches, the effect is close to that of oil painting.

BETWEEN SHOWERS by Margaret Glass

ARTISTS' SANDPAPER

1 *On sandpaper, it is impossible to blend colours in the normal way, so mix colours on the fruit by laying one over another, using positive line strokes. Proceed in the same way on the plate.*

2 *As far as possible, use colours as they come, choosing a selection of blues, greens and red-browns that will look well together.*

3 *Mix some colours on the dish by overlaying, then strengthen the shadows beneath the fruit. Continue slowly building up the colours until you are satisfied with the result.*

PASTEL BOARD

 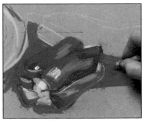 

1 *Pastel board grips the pastel firmly and gives a crisper line than velour paper. Try to exploit this, overlaying colours on the red pepper with a series of lines.*

2 *Add further colours to the pepper to build up the forms, then work on the blue tablecloth, pushing the pastel firmly into the board so that it is completely covered.*

3 *Use firm linear strokes to describe the forms of the pumpkin. There is already a considerable buildup of colour, but the surface has not become clogged, as it would have on standard pastel paper.*

Textured Ground

*All pastel papers have some texture because this is necessary for holding the
pigment in place, and there are various different papers to choose from.
However, you can exploit texture in a more dramatic way by laying your
own textured ground.*

To create this textured ground, you will need acrylic paint or a substance called acrylic gesso (a combination of chalk, pigment and plastic binder), along with a heavy watercolour paper or a piece of board, such as mount board. Put on the paint or gesso with an artist's bristle brush or ordinary paintbrush, aiming for a slightly uneven, striated look. When you lay pastel on top of this ground, you will find that the colour catches on the small ridges, creating intriguing effects. It takes a little practise to discover how the method can be used best, but this is essentially a try-and-see technique.

You can also create a surface rather like that of artist's sandpaper by scattering pumice powder onto hardboard or mount board. You will need to lay a coat of adhesive first. This could be either glue sizing, wallpaper paste, or acrylic medium. When the surface has dried out, it can be coloured with thinned acrylic or watercolour.

ACRYLIC GESSO GROUND

1 *Unless you want to work on a white surface, tint the gesso by mixing it with acrylic paint of a neutral colour. This method is quick because there is only one layer to dry. However, you could apply the gesso first and then tint it.*

2 *Using a bristle brush, paint the coloured gesso all over a piece of heavy watercolour paper. Aim for an uneven effect, because you want the striated texture of the brushstrokes to show through the pastel.*

3 *Allow the gesso to dry. Make a charcoal drawing and then begin to apply colour on the bottles, using bold side strokes and heavy pressure.*

4 *Draw two or three broad strokes of yellow for the corks and begin to work the background around them, using first blue-grey and then white.*

5 *Build up the detail on the bottles with an edge of white pastel. You will not be able to achieve fine lines because the texture breaks up the strokes, so try for broad effects.*

6 *The underlying texture contributes a lively quality, and although detail is limited, the bottles are convincingly rendered. This method is exciting if you do not fight the texture but go with it.*

Gestural Drawing

The essence of this technique is using rapid and uninhibited movements of the pastel to capture the immediate impression of a subject.

Gestural drawing relates particularly well to subjects that have movement – individuals or groups of people, animals, a windswept landscape, or a pounding sea. It is important to develop a free connection between what you observe and the way you translate it to paper, letting the motion of your hand and arm echo the rhythms of shape, contour and direction. The spontaneity of the

MOVEMENT STUDIES by Judy Martin
Sequential movement can be studied in simple outline drawings, letting your hand follow freely the rhythms of the form. Each of these sketches was done in a matter of seconds, as a means of studying the motion rather than aiming for a definite image.

OVER THE JUMP by Judy Martin
An open, linear style has been used to draw the horse and rider, beginning with free outlines that are gradually reworked to refine the shapes. The colour of the paper gives a coherent background to the rapidly laid marks. Broader sweeps of colour are added with side strokes and loose hatching to give the image a sense of depth and solid form.

T'AI CHI EXERCISE by George Cayford

Fluid contour lines capture the essence of the pose and also describe the roundness of the limbs and body, where the artist's hand lets the pastel tip flow easily around the forms. The movement sequence is described here using successive colours as elements of the pose slowly change.

BALLET DANCER by Kay Gallwey

Active treatment of every area of this image enhances the impression of space and form. Directional marks are used to indicate the structure and detail of the background location, to describe the textures of the dancer's dress and hair, and to suggest her movements.

approach is lost if you become concerned with individual details.

Gestural drawing is specially successful with soft pastels or oil pastels because they glide easily across the paper and provide a broad range of surface effects. Exploit your repertoire of linear marks and use loose side strokes to convey massed colour or tone. If you work with hard pastels or pastel pencils, the character of the medium suggests a more sketchy, linear style, using scribbled textures and roughly worked hatching or crosshatching to represent volume and contour.

ALTERNATIVE TECHNIQUES

Wet Brushing

Pastels are normally used dry, but they can be mixed with a variety of binders or with water and spread with a brush. Wet brushing is an excellent way of covering the paper quickly.

USING WATER

1 *Thin paper may buckle when water is applied, so choose Canson Mi-Teintes or watercolour paper. Block in the composition and establish the principal shapes and colours. Use light side strokes for this work.*

2 *Dip a broad bristle brush into clean water and begin to spread the pastel. Once wet, pastel takes on the consistency of paint and fills the grain of the paper with solid colour.*

3 *Wash the brush to remove traces of the paler colour, and spread black pastel on one side of the tree trunk only. This produces a gradation of tone that describes the form; specks of the paper still show through the areas of dry pastel, making it appear lighter.*

USING TURPENTINE

1 *It is safe to use Ingres paper for the turpentine method, since the spirit evaporates and does not cause the paper to buckle. Block in the picture with side strokes, laying one colour over another on the tree trunk to make a soft blend.*

2 *When you are satisfied with the composition and balance of colours, begin the wet brushing, again using a bristle brush but this time dipping it in turpentine. The paper will turn almost black but will resume its normal colour as soon as the solvent dries.*

3 *The turpentine makes the pastel greasier. Work into the still-wet paper with dry pastel and you will find that the colour spreads easily.*

TAOS FALL by Bob Rohm
This work on sandpaper was built up in layers of rich colour over a turpentine-brushed under-painting. The pastel colour was dissolved with turpentine and scrubbed onto the paper.

Resist Techniques

Resist methods are based on the incompatibility of oil- and water-based mediums.

If you lay down lines or patches of colour using an oil pastel, then brush over it with a thin wash of ink, watercolour or acrylic paint, the greasy texture of the pastel repels the fluid colour. The paint settles into the paper around the oil pastel marks, leaving their colour and texture clearly visible. With repeated applications of both media, allowing the washes to dry in between, you can build up a dense, complex image.

A lightweight pastel stroke leaves parts of the paper grain unfilled, so the paint will settle into irregularities within the pastel colour as well as around the edges. To get very distinctive, strong-coloured marks, you need to apply the pastel quite heavily. The best media for this technique if you want to layer the image are inks and liquid watercolours (those sold in bottles).

Some hard pastels have a wax content that makes them of limited use for resist technique. You need to experiment with the range and density of hard pastel marks, as sometimes they do repel the wet colour but also intermittently they absorb it. Soft pastels are ineffective as resist media, as the colour will spread into an overlaid wash (see Wet Brushing on pages 58–59).

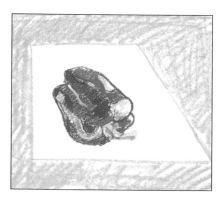

1 *Draw the image in oil pastel using heavy, boldly textured strokes. You can apply as many colours as you wish.*

2 *Apply a free wash of ink or liquid watercolour, using a large, soft brush to flood the colour easily over the pastel drawing.*

3 *As you complete the wash, the liquid colour will settle into the paper grain within and around the pastel marks. You can use a single colour for the overlay, or more than one.*

SCRATCHING OUT (right)
Some particularly dense drawing inks may flood the pastel marks rather than be repelled by them. If this occurs, you can use a knife blade to scratch back the ink when it is dry, retrieving the colour of the underlying image.

LAYERING THE IMAGE (left)
This resist image was built up in several

stages with liquid watercolour over oil pastel. The textured pattern of the leaves was first drawn with white, pink and grey pastels, then loose washes of brown and green watercolour were overlaid. When the paint dried, parts of the pastel drawing were reworked and further washes applied, adding blue and red to the colour range. This process was repeated once again to build up the density of colour and texture.

Scraping Out

Scraping out is a technique that enables you to re-establish a workable surface when you have built up layers of soft pastel very thickly and find it difficult to apply further colour.

A heavy accumulation of pigment particles can be scraped back with the flat edge of a fine blade, such as a scalpel or craft-knife blade. You can then spray the area lightly with fixative and redraw when the fixative has dried.

Some artists use the technique very successfully as a positive drawing element. Scraping out pastel layers has the effect of fusing the colours in a rough, scratchy overall texture; if a coloured ground is used, its underlying shade also becomes meshed into the pastel colour. The texture typically has a linear quality corresponding to the direction in which the blade travels over the surface, which gives additionally a sense of movement.

You have to manipulate the blade carefully to avoid shaving the grain of the paper or digging into the surface. Because of the textural interaction of the medium and support in pastel work, it is very difficult to either disguise or accommodate actual surface damage.

1 *In an area of the composition that is to be reworked, the colour is scraped back using the flat edge of a lightweight craft-knife blade. To avoid damaging the surface, follow the grain of the pastel marks.*

2 *In reapplying pastel colour over the scraped section, the marks are built up with the same consistency and direction as in the surrounding areas.*

LINEAR TEXTURE

Scraping out can be used as a positive element of drawing technique for introducing very fine linear texture in a colour composition. In this example, the tip of a blade has been used to draw into heavily applied colour, creating the whiskery effect of the seedheads and enhancing the complexity of the varied directional lines in the massed grasses.

Frottage

Frottage is a means of reproducing the effect of a specific texture by placing your paper over a textured surface and rubbing the pastel stick over the paper.

The different features of the underlying texture show up as variations in the pastel colour. Whether the surface is raised or recessed at any given point will cause the pressure of the pastel stick to vary and you will automatically obtain corresponding changes of tone from dark to light.

Frottage ranges from subtle, evenly patterned impressions taken from a close-textured material such as hessian or fine metal mesh to the irregular graphic effects thrown up by a coarse wood grain. You can take up a lightly grainy texture from heavy sandpaper, or reproduce the man-made pattern of a sheet of moulded plastic or glass.

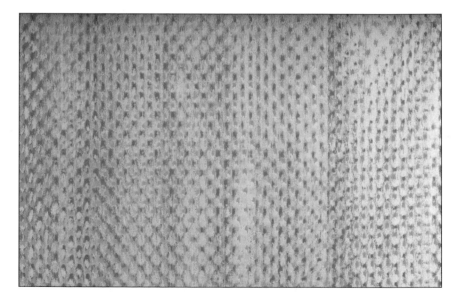

LAYERED COLOURS

Broken colour effects and complex textures can be built up with successive layers of frottaging. This works particularly well with regular textures like a mesh weave or evenly embossed surface. The interwoven effect of this sample is achieved by moving the paper slightly between colours so each application mixes with the one before.

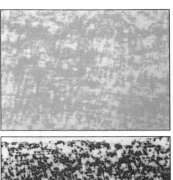

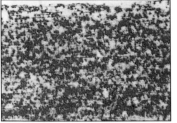

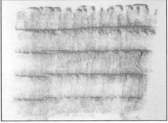

The effects of frottage are unique to each surface, and sometimes unpredictable. The examples here were achieved by rubbing over from (left clockwise): architectural stonework, woodgrain, rough textured concrete and a slatted wooden door.

The character of your rubbing will also depend upon the type of pastel you use. Soft pastels and oil pastels will tend to form a cohesive surface effect, while hard pastels and pastel pencils show stroke marks that may be difficult to eliminate, adding a faint linear bias to the texture picked up from the underlying material. The effects of overlaying pastel colours using the same or different textures is interesting to experiment with as a way of obtaining areas of broken colour.

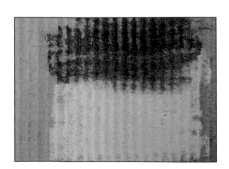

CORRUGATED CARDBOARD
Unusual textures can be particularly effective if suitably matched to a given subject. For example, the ribbed texture of corrugated cardboard could enhance the effect of a landscape or townscape view.

MIXED MEDIA
Charcoal and Pastel

Charcoal is the medium traditionally used for sketching the layout of a composition, providing the guidelines for the application of colour and tone.

Charcoal is a useful complement to pastel, particularly soft pastels and oil pastels, which you might use to build dense impasto effects over a compositional framework drawn with charcoal. You can create a quite clearly defined charcoal sketch to begin with, then brush away the loose charcoal with a soft paintbrush before introducing the colour work.

Alternatively, you can use charcoal as a more significant visual element to enhance the graphic qualities of a pastel drawing. The textures of charcoal and soft pastel go well together, but charcoal is grittier and can contribute sharp line qualities and hard blacks. To avoid contaminating colours with black dust and charcoal fragments, confine this mixed-media approach to quick sketches and studies, and use frequent, very light sprays of fixative as necessary.

PASTEL OVER CHARCOAL

1 *In this example, charcoal is used to create a detailed monochrome drawing of the subject, which then forms a base for the colour rendering. In the initial drawing, sharp lines are contrasted with loosely worked shading and graded tones. When applying the charcoal, you can work up the dark tones quite heavily. Because it is a very dry medium, it does not clog the paper tooth.*

3 *The first layers of colour are blocked in quickly using the tip and edge of the pastel stick. At first, these show broad colour variations across the whole image. Highlights are applied to counterbalance the dark charcoal tones.*

2 *Light and mid-tones can be smoothly graded by rubbing the charcoal with a tissue. Dust off the surface and apply a light spray of fixative before starting to apply pastel colour.*

4 *As the colours are built up more heavily, charcoal is again used where* necessary to redefine the framework of the composition and give emphasis to the forms. It is possible to draw over the pastel and still obtain clean, heavy blacks. In the final stages, the balance of tones is adjusted by applying thick colour with the tip of the pastel stick to develop highlight areas and colour accents.

5 *The finished composition has a strong pattern of light and shade. Foreground shapes remain dark, with the pastel used just to tint the blacks, while the light near the windows is conveyed by heavier outlays of colour, the charcoal showing through as a linear framework.*

67

Gouache and Pastel

Gouache and soft pastel are ideal partners for mixed-media work, providing similar colour character and complementary textures. Both are opaque media in which the pure hues and tints are particularly brilliant. Gouache lightens slightly as it dries, and its paler colours are highly reflective.

In combining these media, let the gouache do the painting and take advantage of pastel's qualities as a drawing medium to provide additional detail and textural contrast. Exploit linear strokes and massing techniques that can be integrated with flat washes of gouache, broad brushmarks, or heavy impasto.

This is an excellent combination of media for outdoor subjects – landscape and townscape. You can block in the general colour areas with gouache and work over them with pastel to develop the textures and patterns of, for instance, grass, flowers and foliage, or building materials and architectural details. Another good use of pastel in this context is for inserting figures after you have established the main features of your outdoor scene, freely drawn over the dried gouache, and for touching in final highlights and colour accents.

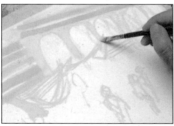

1 *The composition is lightly sketched in with a pale yellow soft pastel. Initially, washes of gouache colour are laid into the background area, blocking in the main forms of the building.*

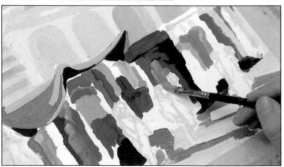

2 *Basic shapes and colours in the market stalls and roadway are similarly blocked in. In these early stages, the main purpose is to eliminate most of the white paper and create a colourful surface for working over in more detail.*

3 The ribbed pattern of the stonework on the left-hand wall is drawn over the dried gouache layer using brown and orange soft pastels. Thicker bands of gouache are overpainted on the same area.

4 The combination of media is freely worked to develop texture and colour overall. With the figures blocked in, all the white paper is now covered, and pastels are used to draw in finer detail on the figures and stalls.

5 Pastel work on and around the figures is quite free and sketchy, but designed to model the forms more solidly and give an impression of greater detail. The grain of the paper is still visible, although the pastel is applied over opaque gouache.

6 Pastel is used to enhance the lights and shadows on the roadway. In the background, the proportions of the wall of arches are adjusted using solid gouache applications and broken dry-brush textures, together with some pastel shading.

Oil Paint and Pastel

Oil pastel can be combined with oil paint to contribute additional linear qualities subtly different from those that can be achieved by brush drawing.

Marks drawn directly onto canvas with oil pastel have a grainy quality that can be retained when lightly overlaid with oil paint thinned to a semi-transparent glaze. Alternatively, you can work into a thin layer of oil paint with the pastel tip to develop linear textures and shading. The passage of the pastel stick actually grooves the surface of the paint and also leaves colour traces.

When you are working into wet paint, the medium or diluent used to thin the paint may soften the pastel texture. If you want to achieve harder line qualities, allow the paint layer to begin drying before you add pastel work.

If you work on paper or cardboard very lightly primed with gesso (or even unprimed), the oil paint will dry very quickly. Because the paper absorbs some of the oil, it will also have a matte surface, which blends well with the pastel.

DRAWING INTO OIL PAINT

2 *The whole image area is covered in the same way, using the paint only at this stage to create a solid rendering of the two bottles and a general impression of the vertical and horizontal planes.*

1 *The basic shapes in the still life are drawn with oil pastel on a primed surface. The main colour values are rapidly blocked in with oil paint applied quite thickly.*

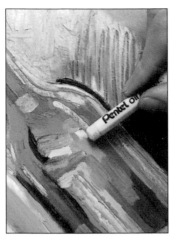

3 Black and grey pastels are used to hatch in the shadow area behind the right-hand bottle. Details of the reflected colours and highlights on the glass are drawn into the wet paint with yellow, green and yellow ochre oil pastels.

4 In the same way, linear details of the pattern on the lace doily are drawn with black and yellow ochre pastels. The pastel tips are sharpened by shaving them with a knife, to produce a fine line.

5 Shading of the background is strengthened with black oil pastel, and the rims and bases of the bottles are more strongly defined with pastel lines and accenting strokes. To enhance the tonal contrasts, white highlights and intense black shadows on the bottle glass are brushed in with bold dabs of solid, opaque paint.

Pencil and Pastel

However dextrous you become in manipulating pastels as drawing tools, it is difficult to sustain a hard, sharp line in this medium.

Some subjects suggest a style of rendering in which linear qualities should be combined with a softer technique – seaspray washing over jagged rocks, for instance, or a bird of prey with a sharp beak and glittering eyes mounted on a mass of rumpled feathers. In such cases, pencils can be a useful complement to pastels.

Choose relatively soft pencils, those graded from B to 6B. In relation to pastels, of course, even these are fine, hard drawing points, yet they produce a subtle variability of line and appreciably grainy texture

that complement pastel qualities. If you are using the pencil only for line work, you can work it into and over pastel colour, and vice versa. If you build up dense pencil shading or hatching, the slightly greasy texture of the graphite will resist an overlay of dry pastel particles.

Use the pencil decisively but delicately. If you allow the point to groove the paper and then try to erase any lines, the impressions will show up through pastel worked over the same area; otherwise, you can combine the media very freely. You

1 *The basic form of the animal is blocked in with soft pastel, using linear marks and broad colour areas rubbed with the fingers.*

2 *A furry texture is built up around the tiger's face with lightweight, feathered strokes of a 2B pencil.*

could explore the combination of line and colour further by trying other point media, such as coloured pencils, felt-tip pens and even pen and ink.

3 *Pencil line is also used to sharpen the detail around the eyes and nose, working freely over the pastel colour.*

4 *As the drawing develops, loose hatching and shading with the pencil builds up the stronger blacks of the tiger's stripes. Variations in the density of the pencil marks create texture and tonal variation.*

Scratchboard and Pastel

You can use oil pastels to make a kind of scratchboard. The effect this gives is very different from that of conventional scratchboard, and it is also quite unlike the marks and impressions you make by drawing directly with the pastel stick.

You begin by building up a layer of solid black on the surface of a piece of smooth-finished artboard, using repeated thin applications of waterproof black India ink brushed on evenly. Once the ink layer is dry, you scribble hard with a white or light-coloured oil pastel so that the surface is covered with a rich, thick, slightly textured layer of colour. Oil pastel tends to adhere unevenly to the smooth surface, so you are bound to get some minor variations of tone and texture, but aim to cover the ink as solidly as you can.

With the pastel layer complete, you can begin to draw into the surface, using a pointed or hard-edged tool – a scriber, the tip of a large nail, or a scalpel blade, for example, or for less sharp effects, the wooden end of a paintbrush. As you scratch into the pastel layer, you reveal the ink, making linear marks that can be true black or greyed, depending on how cleanly you remove the pastel. If you get something wrong, correction is an easy matter; work over the surface again with the pastel and redraw

1 *Use a firm piece of white artboard with a smooth surface that will not buckle when wet. Coat the board with black ink, building up the density with two or three applications, allowing the ink to dry completely at each stage.*

2 *Take the paper wrapping off a stick of white pastel and rub the pastel firmly over the inked surface, gradually covering the board with a thick layer of white.*

with your scratching tool.

This technique corresponds to ordinary methods of drawing in monochrome, except that you are recovering the black marks from the white surface, rather than laying them on. It is similar to sgraffito, but the important factor here is the resilience of the ink surface and the way its density and slight sheen contribute to the final effect of the image.

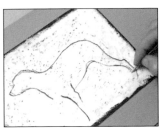

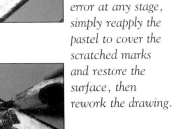

3 *Use any suitable tipped or pointed tool – a large masonry nail is used here – to draw into the oil pastel, scratching it back to reveal the black underneath.*

4 *If you make an error at any stage, simply reapply the pastel to cover the scratched marks and restore the surface, then rework the drawing.*

5 *To remove larger areas of the pastel coating, scrape it back with the edge of a craft-knife blade. Move it flatly across the surface to avoid digging into the board.*

6 *As the drawing becomes more detailed, you can adjust the balance of line and tone and develop the textural variation by reapplying pastel and reworking the scratched lines and shapes as required.*

Watercolour and Pastel

*The translucency and fluidity of watercolour make an interesting
complementary contrast to the opacity and density of soft pastel.*

Both media have brilliant colour
qualities but quite different surface
characteristics. In combination, they
can form images of depth and
subtlety that convey transient effects
of light and shade particularly well.
A mixed-media approach is highly
suitable for interior subjects and
landscapes that include elements of
mood and atmosphere.

The simplest way of combining
these media successfully is to begin
by blocking in the composition with
watercolour washes to establish the
main colour areas and the patterns
of light and shade. Then, when the
watercolour has dried, rework the
whole image in pastel to develop
detail and emphasize colour accents
and tonal contrasts. You can treat this
as a layering process, alternating
watercolour and pastel work and
working the detail more finely at
each stage.

Pastel can also be worked into a
watercolour wash while it is still wet,
or just damp. The granules of the
pastel spread in the moisture,
creating interesting textural effects.

*Pastel and watercolour can be combined in a number of ways. In the picture above, soft
pastel has been applied lightly to watercolour paper with a rough surface. A watercolour
wash is then laid on top so that the speckled marks made by the pastel show through the
transparent paint.*

In this painting of the artist's cat, watercolour was used for the background. A loose wash was laid on dampened, prestretched watercolour paper, which enabled a relatively large area to be covered much more quickly than would be possible with pastel. It has also created an interesting contrast in textures, with the fur of the cat conveyed by the thick build-up of pastel on the grainy surface.

Using Fixatives

To fix or not to fix? That is the question which causes more controversy among pastel artists than any other.

The brilliance and fragility of the pigment particles clinging to the working surface are regarded by some artists as essential characteristics of pastel work. Fixatives may be considered to degrade both the colour and texture of soft pastels. However, careful fixing need not spoil the surface qualities, and you may feel that any disadvantages are offset by the protection that fixative gives to your work, both during its stages of development and when it is finished.

The key to successful fixing is to use the fixative sparingly. Overwetting the surface can cause the pigment particles to merge, muddying the texture; it can encourage strong colours to bleed through overlying tints; and it does tend to darken colours slightly. But if you apply a light layer of fixative at successive stages of the drawing, it enables you to overwork colours freely and keep the hues, tones and individual marks distinct and clean. Fixing again when the work is finished prevents accidental smudging, powdering or flaking.

If you are working on a light- or medium-weight support, you can spray the fixative on the back of the paper. It will penetrate enough to gently dampen the pastel and make it more secure. If you definitely prefer to do without fixative, try fixing the surface of a finished work by laying a sheet of tissue over it and applying even pressure to push the pastel particles a little more firmly into the paper grain.

Aerosol cans of fixative are convenient and are usually now environmentally friendly. Some artists still prefer using a mouth diffuser spray to apply fixative from a bottle, but you do get a more reliably even spray from an aerosol.

Make a quick test spray first to check that the nozzle is clear and the spray quality even. Hold the can about 30 cm (12 in) from the paper and spray from side to side, covering the whole area. Avoid overspraying, as this wets the surface and may cause colours to run or mix.

Making Changes

People who have not used pastel are sometimes discouraged from trying the medium because they have been told that they cannot correct errors. It is true that you cannot erase a pastel line as cleanly as a pencilled one, but there are ways of making corrections, particularly in the early stages.

Although pastel is suitable for both linear drawing and full-colour painting, it is easier to make corrections in the painting mode. Firmly drawn pastel strokes cannot be erased as clearly as can pencil or charcoal ones, though you can partially remove them with a kneaded eraser; if the lines are not too heavy, they may come out successfully. (Never use an ordinary eraser for pastel work; this will simply push the colour into the paper.) The type of paper is another factor; for example, pastel adheres less strongly to standard pastel papers than to sandpaper or pastel board, so it is easier to remove from the standard papers.

If you are building up a painting in layers, you can make corrections at more or less any stage in the work, simply by working over the area with further colours. Because pastel is an opaque medium, the new colours will cover the earlier ones, provided there is not already a thick build-up of pigment. If you find a light colour will not cover a darker one without muddying, this means that you have already filled the grain of the paper, and you will have to remove some colour before working further. This can be done by flicking it off with a stiff brush and then, if necessary, wiping down the area with a rag.

If you find towards the end of a

USING A PIECE OF BREAD

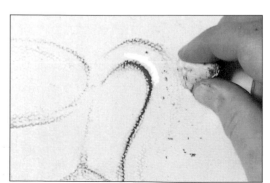

Take a piece of soft white bread and squeeze it between your fingers so that it has the consistency of a putty eraser. Dab the bread onto the surface to lift off the pastel.

picture that there is an area you would like to change, and the pastel is too thick to work over, you can scrape away the top layers of pigment with the flat of a sharp blade and then use a putty eraser. This process, however, should be a last resort because you can easily damage the paper unless you work extremely cautiously. You also run the risk of creating dust that spills onto adjacent areas; so either cover the rest of the surface with paper or pick up the dust with the eraser as soon as you have scraped it off.

USING BRUSH AND COTTON WOOL

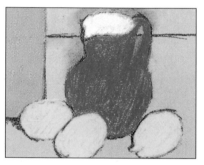

1 *Often you will spot a mistake only after you have blocked in the picture. In this drawing, the ellipse at the top of the jug is incorrect.*

2 *Flick lightly with a bristle brush to remove the top layer of pigment. At this stage the colour has not been pushed into the paper, so it comes away easily.*

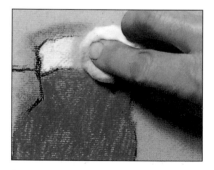

3 *However, to clean the surface sufficiently for reworking, you may need stronger measures, so rub off the remaining colour with cotton wool.*

4 *Redraw the ellipse and fill in with white before continuing to work on the body of the jug.*

OIL PASTEL

Because of the greasy texture of oil pastel, which makes it cling to the paper, it is more or less impossible to erase drawn lines; but you can, to some extent, make corrections by overworking, again providing that the paper grain is not fully filled. If this has happened, it is possible to remove earlier layers of colour by gently wiping with a rag soaked in white spirit (mineral spirits), or for small areas, scrubbing the colour off with a brush. You will be left with a stain on the paper, but this does not matter because it will be covered by the new colours.

USING A BLADE

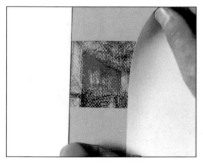

1 *This method is useful for small areas, where the pastel is too thick to work over.*

2 *Scrape the pigment off with the side of a sharp knife, making sure to work gently and carefully to remove the colour layer by layer.*

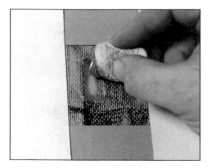

3 *Finally, dab lightly with a putty eraser to pick up the pastel dust. Take care not to press hard or you could smear the remaining colour.*

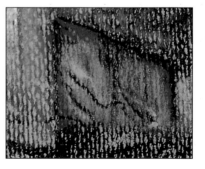

4 *Once the pastel dust is removed, the subtle improvement in the painting can be seen.*

COLOUR AND COMPOSITION

As you gradually develop the range of
colours in a painting or drawing, you will
find that the appearance of individual
colours seems to change each time you
introduce a new element. Colours are
relative – they interact and react to one
another on the working surface.
Composition in drawing and painting is a
fascinating and complex subject, and
many books have been devoted solely to
this one theme, describing the myriad
principles that artists have evolved over
the years for arriving at a successful
result. In this next section we shall
discuss colour and composition in fairly
simple terms, and offer some guidelines
that will hopefully act as springboards for
your own ideas.

COMPOSITION
Planning the Picture

Now that you have practised handling pastels, you can begin to think about the process of organizing – or composing – your painting. There are few hard and fast rules for composition, but there are some helpful general pointers to bear in mind.

Not everything that you see in nature forms the perfect picture, a ready-made composition just waiting to be copied and set down on paper. No matter how breathtaking a view is, you may find that you have to select and re-arrange the elements of the scene in order to arrive at a satisfying pictorial design that continues to hold your interest beyond the first few moments of pleasure. If you simply set up your easel and plunge right into the painting, you will almost certainly live to regret it because the result will lack cohesion and look either bland and boring or confused and unbalanced.

YELLOW ROSE TEXTURE by Maureen Jordan
Floral subjects have a built-in tendency towards symmetry; it is natural to want to place the vase in the middle of the picture so that you can fit all the flowers in. You can do this safely as long as you arrange the flowers themselves in such a way that the symmetry is broken. Here the bottoms of the blooms make an upward-sloping diagonal, and the flower at the top is not placed centrally.

Always look for the main shapes. Here the group of flowers makes a geometric shape that counterpoints the cylinder of the vase.

Each time you approach a subject, start by making sketches and experiment with different viewpoints and arrangements of colour and tone. Try varying the scale of the elements and the relationships between them; and most important of all, decide what you want your picture to say and how best to emphasize what is most important about it.

UNITY AND DIVERSITY

The way to create unity in a picture is by introducing elements that relate to and echo each other, such as the similar shapes of trees, hills and clouds in a landscape, or the rounded forms of fruit, vegetables and jugs in a still life. These visual links have a pleasing effect because the human eye finds related forms more satisfying than unrelated forms.

Tones (areas of light and dark) and colours will also create unity if they are kept within a fairly narrow scale and are connected subtly throughout the composition. Too many different colours and tones, arranged in a haphazard way, will have the opposite effect and leave the viewer feeling confused.

Repeated shapes, like these monoliths, are much more interesting if you stress their lack of uniformity. The artist has paid particular attention to this, stressing it by varying the degree of shadow on each, and he has also chosen an off-centre viewpoint which helps offset the horizontal stretch of fields. Colour, too, has been used to enhance the shape contrasts, the intense yellow of the far-distant field effectively pushing the monoliths into sharp relief.

85

Too much regular repetition, however, has a 'wallpaper' effect and makes for a monotonous picture. So it is necessary to think of ways to introduce diversity without detracting from the overall unity of the composition. For example, repeated shapes will be far more telling if they are not exactly alike but vary slightly in size and outline. A line of trees which are all precisely equidistant will look like a row of soldiers; use a bit of artistic licence and vary the spacing between them. Spaces themselves are an important part of a painting, and should be used in a positive way as shapes rather than just as areas where nothing happens. In a landscape that consists of horizontals, introduce a vertical shape which acts as a counterpoint, or a curved line which leads the eye into the picture.

WEAR THE GREEN WILLOW by Lionel Aggett
The repetitive shapes of the deckchairs form an interesting still-life group, sufficiently varied in their different heights and spacings to avoid a regimented effect. The colour values and directions of the pastel strokes have been expertly controlled to create the subtle translucence of the deckchair fabrics.

ARRANGING THE ELEMENTS

The way in which a picture is divided up makes an immediate impact. It is, therefore, important to think of the picture in terms of abstract shapes, colours and tones, regardless of what the subject matter is. Most pictures, for example, contain a focal point that is supported by other elements which lead the eye towards it, and these elements have to be carefully planned and placed.

Think of your paper as a stage and yourself as stage director in charge of the actors, scenery, props and lighting. Imagine you are directing a dramatic scene. How will you arrange the lighting and scenery to gain maximum impact? How will you position the principal character and the supporting cast?

THE FOCAL POINT

Most pictures contain one main centre of interest – a point to which the viewer's eye is inevitably drawn. A picture that has a main centre of interest will communicate more forcefully than one that does not. But what if your subject contains several objects or areas that are potential focal points? You must determine, first of all, what your picture is about, or what you want to say in it, and then what to stress in order to say it. Stressing, or emphasizing, one element is partly a matter of subordinating the others, such as by keeping a background less detailed and distinct or in a lower colour key. This does not mean that these subordinate areas can be poorly drawn, but rather that the drawing

Set slightly off-centre, the focal point of this picture is the palm plant on its deep blue surface. But the very shape of the palm frond guides our eye to the buildings outside. These have an almost equal intensity of colouring to that of the interior, but we can read them as being outside because of the cool colour of the strong, vertical mullion.

In pastel painting, it is possible to omit the background altogether so that attention focuses solely on the main subject. Unlike other media, the subject can be kept gently 'locked' into the picture space by employing a technique called vignetting. Here the soft strokes of blue picked up from the girl's dress appear to melt and fade into the toned paper. Unity is achieved because the tone of the paper appears to reflect the flesh colours used in the girl's face.

should be firmly understood but not stressed. In a still life, you may wish to place emphasis on a jug of bright flowers and play down the other elements; in a landscape, you can emphasize a dramatic sky by lowering the horizon line so that the land becomes less important by occupying less space; in a portrait, the sitter's face is generally the focus of attention, so you might deliberately tone down the colours and textures of the sitter's clothing, or treat them in broader and more sketchy terms.

In pastel painting it is possible to concentrate solely on the main subject and omit the background altogether, in a technique known as vignetting. The idea is to leave an area of the toned paper around the subject and gently fade out the edges with soft strokes that appear to melt into the surrounding paper. In order to achieve an integrated, harmonious result, it is important to leave areas of untouched paper within the subject as well as around it. For instance, in a portrait the buff-coloured paper can serve as the middle tone for the colours of the flesh. If the subject itself is too thoroughly filled in, it will simply look as though you have forgotten to paint the background.

CHOOSING THE RIGHT FORMAT

Along with the compositional arrangement of the image itself, the size and shape of the paper or board should be considered carefully. With experience, you will come to think of your subject simultaneously with the shape and size of area it is to occupy. For instance, as a general rule, a long, narrow rectangle seems to be the right shape for the broad sweep of a landscape or seascape. A square shape suggests stability, and may be suited to a still life or a close-up study of a single object. An upright format suggests strength and power, and is the usual choice for portraits. But does your view always have to conform to these rules? Might it not be as effective to place a rectangle on end to make it vertical, and thus create a more arresting view of a seascape?

Size is also important. It can have a strong effect on the way a person works and, therefore, on the finished result. A large piece of paper may seem the right choice for a broad, atmospheric seascape, whereas a small one can be ideal for a still life or flower piece in bright, jewel-like colours. But although it can be enjoyable to experiment with different shapes and sizes, a good compromise for beginners is to work with a reasonably sized sheet and start the painting or drawing well within it. This allows room to expand and develop the painting outwards in any direction, and avoids constraints imposed by the proportions of the paper.

AUTUMN LIGHT by Lois Gold

In this landscape format painting, the river draws the eye into the picture and divides the foreground into angular shapes. The interplay of shapes is the artist's theme, and she has emphasized it by avoiding detail. Solid blocks of colour have been built up by blending so that individual strokes are barely visible.

Basics of Picture Making

There are two kinds of sketches: those that are finished art in themselves and those that are intended as a basis for paintings.

Sketching for a painting should be regarded as note-taking; the type of notes you make will depend on the medium you are using. Pencil is an excellent and highly versatile sketching tool which can record linear outlines and areas of tone. But, of course, it is monochromatic, so you will either have to make a separate colour sketch or add written markings to the pencil sketch, a common practice among artists. There is nothing more frustrating than pinning up a series of pencil sketches a week after they were made, only to find them useless because you have no idea what the colours were.

Making accurate colour notes involves recognizing colours and describing them meaningfully to yourself. It is no good just writing down 'blue' or 'green'. This will mean nothing to you when you want to use the sketch, but 'very dark blue-green' or 'pale grey-blue with a hint of mauve' will. Some artists use a familiar reference to aid their memory, for example, 'creamy coffee' or 'Chinese-vase blue'. Constructing colour notes is a highly personal activity.

If you are using pastel as your sketching medium, you can place the

CASOLE D'ELSA by David Cuthbert
Coloured pencil is another good medium for making colour sketches. As you can see from this study, you can achieve considerable depth of colour. This could be used as the basis for a finished painting.

emphasis on recording the colours, but you may then find you have insufficient information on shapes and forms.

Look at your sketch critically when you have completed it, and see whether you think you could paint from it. If not, then make another, perhaps in pencil or pastel pencil, concentrating on whatever is missing from the first sketch. It will take practice before you get it right, but once you start working from sketches you will quickly discover what you want from this preliminary information-gathering and the best way to achieve it.

ROOFTOPS, VAUCLUSE by Joan Elliott Bates

If you like to work up finished paintings from on-the-spot sketches, you might consider buying a small box of oil pastels. These are less messy to use than soft pastels because they do not produce dust and they require no fixing.

PAINTING FROM SKETCHES

The painting on the left brings together a series of separate elements, all of which were sketched in advance to provide a visual reference file.

EXPLORING THE OPTIONS

There are decisions to be made at every stage of a painting. As you paint, consider how best to exploit your pastel marks and how much detail to include. Assess your painting to check and adjust the balance of tones and colours. Many of these decisions become instinctive, but there are other, more conscious choices to make before you begin to paint.

Planning a painting is a process of exploring options. The first concerns format (see page 89) and the second, composition. How will you place the subject on the paper, and how much of it will you show? Finally, which colour paper would be the best choice? To guide you through the possibilities, these next four pages show how a professional artist approaches such choices. She has made some quick sketches to help her decide on format and composition, and has then painted the same scene on two different shades of paper to discover how the ground colour influences the overall colour scheme.

A vertical format could work well, allowing the artist to exploit the trees' upward sweep

When working from a photograph, do not automatically adopt the same format. Explore possibilities by masking different areas with four strips of paper.

A horizontal format centres the path. It could be made squarer, thus losing some of left and right sides.

WORKING ON BROWN PAPER

Medium brown is an easy colour to work on. Neutral and therefore unobtrusive, it allows light and dark colours to show up well.

WORKING ON BLUE PAPER

This is a popular choice for landscapes. Touches of blue are often apparent in green foliage, so areas of paper can be left uncovered.

1 *The artist likes to build up her colours with a layering technique. She wants to give the sky and the path a warm tinge, so after making a charcoal underdrawing, she begins with an orange-brown pastel.*

1 *Because this paper is a dark, positive colour, the artist chooses a light pastel for the sky. She needs to block in the light tones early, or the painting might become too low-key.*

2 *Before beginning to assess and adjust tones and colours, the artist covered the entire paper rapidly. The painting is now blocked in, with a definite tonal structure.*

2 *Here you can see how the paper colour influenced both the choice of colours and the way of working. The covering of pastel is lighter than in the other picture, with more of the ground colour coming through to contribute to the effect.*

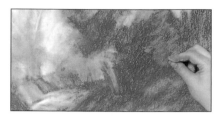

3 The artist develops the colours gradually, moving from one area of the picture to another. Here sides strokes of light green are mixed into the earlier colours and the charcoal drawing to produce a semi-blend.

3 Colours respond to the changing needs of the painting rather than depicting the subject literally. This red-brown adds warmth to the tree and contrasts well with the blue paper.

4 The picture is a broad impression, meaning that detail was not added, but here a little definition is needed. The painting was sprayed with fixative, and a sharp edge of black pastel is used to draw the tree trunk and branches.

4 Because some blue paper will be left showing, the strokes in this painting are placed farther apart, making them more distinct. Here the pastel is applied thickly, but on the path above the artist's hand the paper is visible between strokes.

5 Finally, the sky was lightened, with drifts of yellow suggesting foliage against the light, and a few twigs are drawn with delicate strokes of the pastel edge.

5 Although the specks of blue paper are effective in places, they could detract from this solid dark area. The artist uses her fingers to push the colours firmly into the grain of the paper.

BROWN PAPER

6 *The two paintings have strong similarities, because both are by the same artist, but there are important varitions. The colours are warmer in this version because the brown paper set the colour key.*
The compositions are different, also. Here, the artist cropped some of the foreground and played more with the light and shade on the right side of the path.

BLUE PAPER

6 *When you work on a coloured paper, you need to be assertive in your use of colour. Hence the tonal contrasts are stronger in this painting than in the brown version. This resulted in greater detail and definition. The large tree, for example, gives a clearer suggestion of texture and individual forms. Here, the right-hand foreground is less important than the forceful curve of the path.*

95

WORKING WITH COLOUR

It is difficult to talk about colour in terms of rules and theories, or right and wrong; nevertheless, it is important to have some understanding of how colours behave and how they relate to each other.

Colour is one of the painter's most potent means of expression, and you can use it to emphasize the mood of your painting, thus creating an emotional response in the mind of the viewer. For example, you can use contrasting or vibrant colours to create a strong, dramatic image, or soft, harmonious colours to create a subtle and evocative one.

The specific qualities of certain colours also evoke emotional reaction. Colours such as red and orange are associated with warmth and sunshine, and generally create a positive response, whereas cool colours, such as blue and green, are more passive, associated with misty days and the cool of evening.

Whether your intention is to match colours, tones and textures exactly or to recreate a broad impression of your visual sensations, the properties of the medium will govern what you are able to do.

This next section looks at how colours react together and at the many ways in which they can be used effectively in your pastel paintings.

The Language of Colour

When considering the effects of colour, it is useful to know something about their individual properties and characteristics and to understand what is meant by the various terms used to describe them.

THE COLOUR WHEEL

The colour wheel is a theoretical device which can be referred to when experimenting with colours and the ways in which they react with each other. It is really just a simplifed version of the spectrum, bent into a circle. In the colour wheel below, for example, you can see how those colours that are next to each other tend to harmonize, while colours on opposite sides of the wheel, called complementary colours, are sharply contrasting. The complementary relationships continue around the colour wheel so that, for example, yellow-green is complementary to red-purple and blue-purple to yellow-orange.

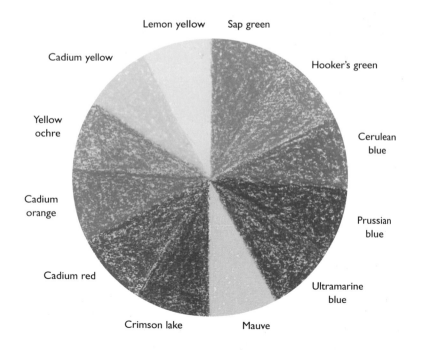

Lemon yellow

Sap green

Cadium yellow

Hooker's green

Yellow ochre

Cerulean blue

Cadium orange

Prussian blue

Cadium red

Ultramarine blue

Crimson lake

Mauve

A Personal Palette

THE ARTIST'S PALETTE

COLOUR COMBINATIONS

Titanium white

Lemon yellow

Ultramarine + Lemon yellow

Cadmium yellow

Yellow ochre

Ultramarine + Viridian

Raw sienna

Raw umber

Cadmium red + Titanium white

Alizarin crimson

Cadmium red

Mauve + Lemon yellow

Ultramarine

Viridian

Raw umber + Cadmium yellow

Mauve

Payne's grey

Yellow ochre + Cadmium yellow

Lamp black

PRIMARY COLOURS

Red, yellow and blue are known as the primary colours because they cannot be made by mixing other colours – they simply exist. Theoretically, it is possible to mix every other colour from the three primaries, but in reality this does not work. You cannot, for example, obtain a true violet by mixing a primary red and blue.

SECONDARY COLOURS

When any two primary colours are mixed together, they form a secondary colour. For example, blue + yellow = green, red + yellow = orange.

TERTIARY COLOURS

These are made by mixing a primary and secondary colour. For example, red + orange = red-orange; yellow + green = yellow-green; blue + violet = blue-violet.

COLOURS WORKING TOGETHER

These samples show how colours look different according to those that surround them. In the top three blocks, the orange stands out well against the more neutral grey-green, and also against the black, which also provides a contrast of tone. In the central block, it makes less impact than the surrounding red. In the bottom three blocks, the cerulean blue looks vivid against the grey-green but less so against the orange-red and the cobalt blue.

COLOUR RELATIONSHIPS

The temperature of a colour is also influenced by neighbouring colours. Have you ever chosen a house paint colour from a small swatch, painted a wall with it, and found afterwards that it looked entirely different? This is an important painting lesson – no colour exists in isolation. The colour appears to have changed because you are now seeing it in the context of accompanying colours – of carpets, curtains and so on.

The same applies to painting with pastels, which will look warmer, cooler, brighter or more muted according to adjacent hues. If you put a bright red or orange against a grey background, for example, it will have more impact than it would if it were placed on yellow or another red. Sometimes a colour will have too much impact. For example, a blue chosen for the distant hills in a landscape will not recede properly, even though it is a cool colour, unless the foreground colours are more vivid and substantially warmer.

Bear the idea of these colour relationships in mind as you work, and you will quickly learn how to play off one colour against another and set up the kind of exciting contrasts that make painting such a rewarding activity.

BACKGROUND COLOURS

FROSTY MORNING by Alan Oliver

The blues used for the distance push the background away, giving a strong sense of space. The artist has chosen a relatively warm blue, but it is still much cooler than the russets and red-browns adopted for the central group of trees and the foliage in the immediate foreground.

Temperature

If you look at the colour wheel, you will see that the red/orange/yellow half appears 'warm' in relation to the other half, whereas the violet/blue/green half appears 'cool'. The reasons for this are partly scientific and partly psychological; we associate reds, oranges and yellows with the sun and firelight, and blues and greens with the coolness of grass and water.

In addition, warm colours tend to come forward, whereas cool colours appear to recede when placed near warm colours.

Within these broad categories, we find that each colour group itself has varying degrees of warmth or coolness. Thus, in the red group, cadmium red is warmer than alizarin crimson, which contains a percentage of cooling blue. Similarly, yellow ochre is a relatively warm yellow because it contains some red, whereas lemon yellow veers towards green and appears cooler.

Although the theory and its terminology needs to be understood, the really interesting part is learning how to apply it to the actual paintings.

WARM AND COOL PRIMARIES

WARM

COOL

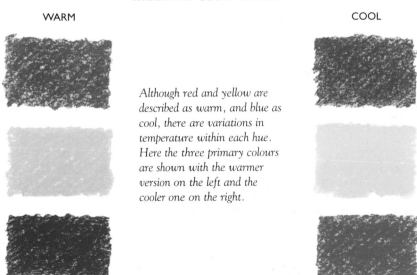

Although red and yellow are described as warm, and blue as cool, there are variations in temperature within each hue. Here the three primary colours are shown with the warmer version on the left and the cooler one on the right.

The effects of bright sunlight in an airy, well-lit room are conveyed beautifully here by the warm, glowing colours the artist has used. She has chosen a warm yellow-grey paper to work on, and has allowed it to show through in places, thus making links between the different parts of the picture. Notice how she has used bands of complementary colours – blue and yellow – on the tablecloth to give a shimmering effect.

The effect of this pastel of a poppy field in France is charmingly spontaneous, but, in fact, the colours have been used both deliberately and cleverly to suggest space and recession as well as light and warmth. The red poppies, being the warmest colour, advance to the front of the picture and dominate it, while the cooler, hazier blues and pinks of the hills recede into the distance, just as they do in nature.

Harmony and Mood

A picture painted with a limited range of harmonizing colour generally has a calm, restful appearance. There are no jarring colour notes, just subtle changes from one hue to another, and this creates a unified, well-balanced image.

Bear this in mind also when deciding what sort of mood you want to convey in your painting; for example, a portrait of a wistful young girl could be painted in harmonious colours to emphasize a feeling of quiet introspection, whereas a portrait of an active child might be better suited to a more lively colour composition. Similarly, harmonious colours in a landscape express a mood of calm and tranquillity.

In pastel painting, the colour and tone of the paper can play a vital role in lending harmony and unity to a painting. When painting a seascape, for instance, I like to work on a blue-toned or grey-toned paper, with loose pastel strokes that allow the paper to show through and act as a unifying element that ties the other colours together.

There is a risk, of course, that too much harmony can make for a rather bland, insipid painting. One way to avoid this is to include a small area of contrasting colour; for example, a painting with a predominant theme of blue might benefit from a touch of a brighter colour such as pink or yellow.

The range of pale colours here is very closely controlled, with each one blending almost imperceptibly into the one next to it. There is the minimum of contrast in tone or in colour. Harmonious colours do not necessarily have to be pale and delicate, as these are. They can equally be dark or strong; the harmony comes from their close relationship on the colour wheel.

Judging Tonal Value and Neutral Colours

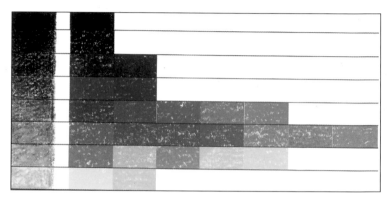

JUDGING VALUE

If you are using the recommended starter palette, become familiar with the value of all the colours by making a chart like this one. Prepare a grey scale with seven shades of grey, then draw up a grid and place a swatch of each colour where it seems to fit in terms of value. This will help you to assess the values in your subject.

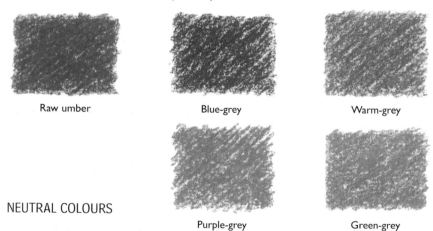

Raw umber

Blue-grey

Warm-grey

Purple-grey

Green-grey

NEUTRAL COLOURS

These are just a few from the large range of so-called neutral colours produced by pastel manufacturers. However, they all have a definite colour bias and must be used with care, since they could look quite bright in a painting that has a muted colour scheme.

PINK ROSES by Maureen Jordan

Most of the colours in this delicate painting can be described as neutral, but because the most vivid ones – those of the roses – are not strong in terms of either hue or tone, the greys, green-greys and rich browns are perceived as having more colour than they might in another setting.

NEUTRALS IN CONTEXT

There are only three genuinely neutral colours: black, white and grey made from a mixture of the two. A colour with any kind of bias will be affected by surrounding colours; these swatches show how two greys behave in different circumstances.

Against red and orange, grey-green appears neutral.

Surrounded by a genuinely neutral grey, made from black and white, grey-green becomes positive.

Purplish grey is much less vivid than blue and pink.

Similarly, the purplish bias of this grey shows up as colour against genuinely neutral grey.

Colour, Tone and Mood

Some colours are warm and appear to advance, whereas others are cool and appear to recede. Using these properties of projection and recession, it follows that you can use warm and cool colours to model form by emphasizing the projecting and receding planes of an object.

You can also create the illusion of three-dimensional depth and space, particularly in landscapes. Once again, nature is your tutor in the use of warm and cool colours; looking across a stretch of landscape, compare the cool, blue cast of trees in the distance with the warmer, more intense greens of those close to you. By capturing that colour difference in a landscape painting, you will achieve a convincing sense of space and depth, because the eye perceives cool colours as being farther away than warm colours.

Warm and cool colours, because of their associations, can also be harnessed to help you express a particular mood. Warm colours suggest exuberance, optimism, passion and cheerfulness. Cool colours, on the other hand, suggest calm, restraint, aloofness, loneliness and sadness. Once again, these general rules shouldn't be taken as gospel; they are meant as starting points for your own ideas about colour.

TONAL VALUES

The ability to analyze the relative tones of a subject and match them in your painting is very important. Yet tone is a concept which gives many artists problems, amateurs and professionals alike. There is a much larger range of tones in life than in pastels. The tones around us range from 1–100, whereas those in paint range only from 1–40. You therefore have to make some tones equivalent in your painting. Just remember that tone doesn't refer to the colour itself but to how light or dark it is in comparison to the colours surrounding it. The tone of a colour cannot be assessed in isolation because it has no existence except in the context of other tones.

The best way to judge the tones of your subject is to look for a neutral middle tone – say, the grey of a sky or the soft green backdrop in a still life – and compare the rest of the tones to this to see if they appear darker or lighter. Keep your eyes moving all the time, from one tone to another and back again. If

Unlike the atmospheric study, right (see also on page 103), the sketch above makes dramatic use of tonal contrasts, or lights and darks. The subject is an olive grove in Crete, where the sun is strong and the shadows very distinct, and the artist has played up the contrasts by using complementary colours as well as tone. Dark blue paper has been used as the main shadow tone, while yellow, which is the complementary of blue, forms the light area of sunlit grass.

you still have difficulty in judging the relative tones, try the old trick of half-closing your eyes. This cuts out most of the colour and extraneous detail, and reduces the scene to shapes of light and dark.

Complementary Colours

Any two colours diagonally opposite each other on the colour wheel are called complementaries. For example, blue is the complementary of orange, red of green and yellow of violet. The complementary of a secondary colour such as red-orange is blue-green, and so on. Complementary colours need to be carefully controlled in order to be successful in a painting, but when used wisely they have great dramatic impact.

INTENSIFYING WITH COMPLEMENTARY COLOURS

If two complementary colours of the same tone are placed near each other, they intensify each other by colour contrast. Though you're not physically aware of it, the eye jumps rapidly from one colour to the other, causing an optical vibration that makes the colours appear to shimmer.

If complementary colours are used in large amounts and in equal proportions, however, the effect will be crude and garish. The secret is to create a web of small flecks of broken colour, as the Impressionists did, so that the overall effect is harmonious.

Or you can use a small patch of a complementary colour to counterbalance a large area of a particular colour (notice how vibrant red poppies appear when growing in a green field, for example). Yet another method is to tone down both colours with their complementaries; for example, if you're painting a bowl of red apples against a green background, introduce flecks of green into the apples and flecks of red into the background – the colours will still intensify each other, but the overall effect will be more subdued.

NEUTRALIZING WITH COMPLEMENTARIES

When complementary colours are used next to each other, they intensify each other. Conversely, if they are mixed together they cancel each other out and form neutral greys and browns. For example, violet and yellow mixed together form grey, and red and green make brown. Depending on which colours are used and the proportions of each, you can create a wide range of colourful neutrals – blue-greys, brown-greys, red-browns, grey-browns, and so on. Mixing all three primary colours together also produces a neutral grey. In the case of pastels, mixing will, of course, take the form of blending or scumbling, but the theory applies equally to pastels and paints.

A word about mixing and blending complementaries: On the whole, an optical mixture, that is, one that mixes in the viewer's eye, appears more vibrant than a physically blended mixture. In other words, if you apply a layer of red and then scumble over it with green, you create a lively brown because the two colours each retain something of their identity and there is inherent movement within the colour. The same applies if you use dots of colour next to each other, as the Pointillists did. Compare scumbled or dotted colour to a flat, smoothly blended area of red and green and you'll see what I mean. Neutral colours don't have to be uninteresting. They should be subtle, but still lively; they are a necessary foil to more brilliant colours. The beauty of pastels is that since they cannot be pre-mixed, as paints are, you will achieve such effects without really trying.

Although the colours here are very muted, to suggest space and distance, complementaries – red and green – have been used in the foreground to bring the poppies to the front of the picture. Without the splashes of red, the picture would have lacked definition and interest.

This bright flower piece provides an interesting contrast to the gentle landscape. Here the colours have been deliberately heightened, and two pairs of complementaries – red and green, and yellow and blue – are set against one another to create a vibrant colour scheme.

COMPLEMENTARY COLOURS IN SHADOWS

To create a feeling of light and luminosity in your paintings, it is essential to notice the colour in the shadows. If you look closely at a cast shadow, especially on a sunny day, you'll see that it may contain a touch of the complementary colour of the object that is casting the shadow. So if you're painting a red vase, for example, try adding a little green to the colour of the cast shadow; if the object is yellow, add a little blue-violet.

On the subject of colourful shadows, there is a fascinating story about Eugène Delacroix (1798–1863), the great nineteenth-century French painter. Delacroix was dissatisfied with the lack of emphasis in some yellow drapery he was painting. Deciding to go to the Louvre to see how Rubens had tackled the problem, he looked for a hackney cab. At that time, around 1830, the Paris cabs were painted canary yellow. When Delacroix spotted one, parked in the sun, he suddenly noticed the violet shadow underneath it. Fired with inspiration, he hastily paid the cabman and returned to his studio to paint violet shadows in the yellow drapery. The result? A masterpiece!

Creating Depth Using Colour

Objects appear more blurred and indistinct the farther away they are, and the tonal differences become much smaller; thus, in a painting of a distant landscape, space and recession can be conveyed by softening the forms of trees or hills on the horizon and blending them into the colour of the sky.

PIGEONS IN THE CAMPO BANDIER E MORO *by Diana Armfield*
The lack of strong detail in the foreground area allows our eye to travel unhindered to the group of figures in the middle distance.

Colour Perspective

In reality, everything around us is three dimensional; in drawing and painting, however, we work on a two dimensional surface. We have to observe objects as if they were flat, like our paper or canvas.

Changing the way we look at objects isn't easy because we tend to think of objects as they are in a diagrammatic form, straight in front of our eyes, like a building in an architectural drawing. In reality, we usually see things from an angle, rather than from straight ahead. From an angle, a round chair or plate looks elliptical; a square appears to lose all its right angles. Horizontal lines appear to slant upwards or downwards; all forms look smaller and smaller the farther away they are. You should, by this time, be keenly aware of these facts. If you are the slightest bit vague on this issue, review basic drawing techniques.

Colour perspective, which refers to changes caused by distance and atmospheric conditions, doesn't seem to have been grasped by artists until the late Middle Ages, when we first see an attempt at indicating distance by employing blue tones in the far background of paintings. Even then, the blue was the same all over a small section of the picture, with every fine detail carefully drawn and painted. All around this small segment of bluish scenery, the painting was always equally strong in colour, without any gradual diminishing of values towards the far background.

IS COLOUR PERSPECTIVE IMPORTANT?

The biggest role of colour perspective is generally in landscape painting, because greater distances and spatial problems are encountered in these subjects than in figure painting. Nonetheless, even in figures and portraits, the background is important, whether it is a plain backdrop of colour, such as a wall or curtain, or a more definite and complex background, such as the interior of a room, a garden, or the kind of romantic scenery Leonardo da Vinci painted behind the *Mona Lisa*. A background, whatever its nature, must look like something behind the figure – not as if the figure were pasted on a sheet of cardboard or, worse yet, as if the figure were merely looking through a hole in a wall or in a curtain.

UNTITLED by David Prentice

Unusual effects of light and shade in landscape derive from the lie of land and transient effects such as cloud shadows. Here the darkened hillside dramatically foreshadows its sunlit neighbour. In keeping with the ambitious scope of the landcape, this pastel painting is on a relatively large scale, at 55 x 85cm (22 x 34in). This allows for the full interplay of the broad sweeps of colour and accommodates the startling sense of scale.

SEPTEMBER EVENING
by Aubrey Phillips

The artist made subtle use of perspective by bringing the curves of the waves closer together as they recede. But it is the tiny figures at the far end of the beach that really suggest its depth and give a sense of distance; they are hardly more than dots and dashes in comparison with those in the middle ground.

The Importance of Values in Colour Perspective

In colour perspective, grasping and perceiving values is of the utmost significance. You may follow all the rules of linear perspective but still make a mess of your painting by neglecting colour values.

A shadow on a tree, on a house, on a road, or on any object isn't merely darker than the rest; it's darker depending on the nearness or distance of the object. The brightest light on a green lawn that's at a distance is not as brilliant as on the same kind of lawn near you. Not only are colours less bright in the distance, they are also more bluish in tone.

Compare the tones farthest away with the tones near you, and paint the shades between the two extremes proportionately. Applying the very darkest, and the very lightest shades first is an excellent way to start your painting. Bear in mind that warm colours appear to advance, while cool colours recede. The more intense the warm colour, the closer it comes to you; the less intense the cool colour, the farther away it moves from you. Add a touch of red, orange or burnt sienna to any colour, and it will come forwards. Add a touch of white, blue or green to any hue, and it will move backwards. You have absolute control over colours.

AVOID HOLES AND JUMPING-OUT COLOURS

Colours in the distance painted as bright as the same hues nearer to you seem to be 'jumping out of the picture' or look as if someone has pasted bright pieces of paper on it, perhaps mischievously. Even the casual onlooker feels that something is wrong with the picture.

Dark sections painted just as dark in the distance as similar objects in the foreground appear to be holes or gashes in the picture. They're fine if you want to paint actual holes or gashes; they're utterly wrong, however, if the dark hue is an accident, based on an oversight or a lack of understanding. Art students often paint tree trunks and shadows under the trees in the same colours and values in the farthest distance as those nearby. Such trees and shadows appear to be standing in one row across the picture, rather than in depth as the artist had planned. And even real holes in the distance must be lighter in value than similar holes nearby.

Although these facts are most

HASTINGS BEACH by Alan Oliver

The colour effects in this atmospheric seascape are subtle, yet no blending has been used. Short strokes slightly varied in direction express shimmering light and movement of sea. Light diagonal hatching over darker colour of boats prevents an over-solid, static appearance; the same method was used on quay and crane. The foreground is treated lightly, with different shapes and sizes of marks suggesting pebbles and fragments of driftwood. Fine lines, such as the masts and the highlights on the edges of the boats, were drawn in the final stages with a sharp edge of pastel.

notable and damaging in realistic subjects, they're just as disturbing in abstract or nonobjective paintings. An artist working in any of these contemporary styles may wish to suggest a big hole, or something sticking out of the painting. Such colour effects can then be utilized for aesthetic purposes.

DOMINANT FOREGROUNDS

WHERE THE SPOTTED OWL FLEW by Doug Dawson

The artist has deliberately limited both his palette and his tonal range in order to convey the peaceful feeling of this woodland, but the colours used for the foreground area are warmer than the greens, blues and pale mauves of the foliage beyond.

POPPIES by Alan Oliver

The foreground is the main subject of this picture. The artist chose a low viewpoint from which the stems and flowers seem to push skywards. Their upward sweep is emphasized by the inclusion of the tall trees and by the direction of the pastel marks. The marks veer to the right in the foreground and to the left in part of the background, enlivening the composition.

SPACE THROUGH PERSPECTIVE

FEN LANDSCAPE
by Geoff Marsters

Perspective makes receding parallel lines appear to draw closer together until they finally meet. In landscapes, such lines are unlikely to be perfectly straight, but they still converge in the distance, and observing this effect correctly will help you create the illusion of space. In this picture, the lines emphasize the depth of the field and also depict the irregularities of the ground.

FALL ON THE FLATLAND by Doug Dawson
Here, the bright patch of water and grass in the centre draws the eye and leads in from the foreground to background, but warm-cool contrasts have also been used. The yellow-green of the left-hand tree stands out against the cooler grey-green, and both colours are close in tone.

Perspective

Whether your subject is one building or an urban panorama, you will have to come to grips with the basic rules of perspective. But these are not really alarming, and once you have mastered them you will find them helpful.

Earlier in this chapter you saw how things appear smaller the farther away they are. This is the starting point of all perspective. If you look at a table-top from the front, you will notice that the sides seem to angle inwards, making the back shorter than the front. This is because all parallel lines receding from you seem to converge, becoming closer together until they meet at a point known as the vanishing point.

The vanishing point is located on an imaginary line called the horizon, a word often used loosely to describe the division between land and sky or sea and sky, but in perspective it has a more precise meaning. The horizon line is your own eye level, so it changes according to where you are, becoming higher when you are standing and lower when you sit. It is important to understand this, because the horizon dictates the angle at which the converging parallel lines slope.

Your angle of viewing also affects the way the parallel lines behave, because the vanishing point is opposite you. If you stand in the

PLOTTING PERSPECTIVE LINES

When making your preliminary drawing, sketch in the horizon line, then draw one of the receding horizontal lines – you could begin with a roofline or the tops of windows. Take this line down to the horizon (H) and mark where the two lines meet. This is your first vanishing point (VP). All the lines parallel with this will meet at the same place.

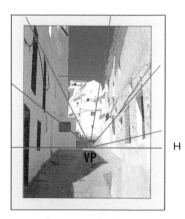

SINGLE VANISHING POINT Here there is only one vanishing point for the buildings, because the viewpoint is the middle of the street. Although the houses are built on level foundations, the road runs uphill, so the vanishing point is above the horizon.

middle of a railway line, it will be directly in the centre, but if you move to one side, it will move to a different point on the horizon line.

Similarly, if you look at a building from an angle, so that each side forms a separate plane, there will be two vanishing points, one for each plane. A complex grouping of buildings set at haphazard angles to one another will have many different vanishing points; but provided you remember that each one is situated at your own eye level, you will not go far wrong.

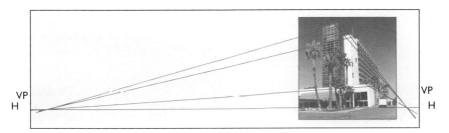

VP
H

VP
H

TWO VANISHING POINTS You can see two separate planes of this building, and each one has its own vanishing point, but at the same level – the horizon line.

MULTIPLE VANISHING POINTS For a subject like this, with buildings set at odd angles to each other, you cannot mark in each vanishing point. But do mark the horizon, and plot the perspective of the foreground buildings.

H —

ELLIPSES

Circles are also affected by perspective, flattening out and becoming ovals. These ellipses often cause confusion, but the principle of foreshortening is the same as for other objects. Just as a book will become shorter when you look at it sitting down, so will the top of a cylinder, or the opening of a mug or vase. From above you will see a near circle, but the ellipse will become progressively shallow as your eye level lowers, until it ceases to be an ellipse and becomes a straight line.

Light and Shadow

Variations of tone model form, create space and contribute mood and atmosphere in painting. The pattern of light and shadow explains where the light is coming from and how strong it is; it modifies the effects of local colour and imposes many active and exciting variations on the basic elements of shape and colour in a subject.

In your painting, these may appear as strong contrasts of hue and tone that create depth and drama, or gentle tonal gradations that model subtle planes and curves or convey the great distances of open landscape. Or you may choose a high-key interpretation of a subject, emphasizing the quality of light by using light tones, or create a harmonious effect by a restricted tonal range that works on related values and eliminates extreme contrasts.

Keep in mind that tone functions two ways in relation to colour. It can be the equivalent of a mono-chromatic scale on which individual colours can be given a range of tonal variation from light to dark – as if mixed with varying degrees of white or black. Or it can be a natural inclination of certain types of hues, or of specific paint colours: Yellows are naturally light colours; reds generally middle-toned; violets and purples typically dark.

TONAL MODELLING
Modelling is the important means by which painters impart a quality of three-dimensional realism into two-dimensional images. A sculptor builds up clay or plaster to develop three-dimensional form, while the painter uses the tonal range of the palette to model an impression of planes and curves, recesses and hollows, solid forms and the spaces between them. This approach is familiar from drawing, where the greys and blacks applied with a pencil or stick of charcoal must stand for all colours and tones, the white of the paper providing high points of illumination. You can use a corresponding grey-scale approach when working with colours, or you can make use of the interactions of variable hues and neutral colours to create space and form.

CAST SHADOWS
Cast shadow, the kind of shadow that your figure throws onto the ground on a bright summer's day, is an absence of light; but in painting it need not mean absence of colour. Tonal contrast is usually more emphatic with cast shadows than in the shadowed gradations that model shape and form: cast shadows may

be hard-edged shapes that cut right across an otherwise strongly illuminated area.

THE LIGHT SOURCE

The tonal framework of an image underpins the colour interactions. You may find that a painting is not working because it lacks a strong enough arrangement of tonal values, however carefully you have considered the scheme of colour. This does not necessarily mean employing a very full and detailed tonal range: the entire palette of many highly successful paintings occupies quite a limited section of the tonal scale. But there is a balance to be sought, whether you are employing high-contrast values or subtle mid-tones.

Tonal structure derives directly from the subject in front of you. Although you can exaggerate or underplay it to a certain degree, there is no point in attempting an interpretation so different that it requires you to imagine a pattern of light and shade. Directional light, whether indoors or out, produces variable contrasts and a fairly complex arrangement of broken shapes. A flood of even lighting from a central source smooths out some of the tonal modelling in a subject and may also flatten colour variations. Conversely, a small, contained light source dramatically illuminates strong contours while darkening internal shapes and obscuring detail in surrounding elements.

DECKCHAIRS AND PARASOLS
by David Napp

An intense, striking colour range like this needs to be anchored by a balanced sense of composition. The large shapes of the umbrellas and their cast shadows, solidly blocked in with cold blues, greens and purples, give weight to the picture and hold down the busy pattern of hot colours across the centre.

Harmony and the Effect of Light on Colour

Natural illumination is provided mainly by the sun. The moon merely reflects the light of the sun with a soft glow, which is harmless to the eye, although Old World superstition warns you not to gaze into the full moon, least you lose your mind!

The stars never hurt your eyes. You can see fairly well by moonlight as your eyes become gradually accustomed to it; and you can behold a vast panorama on a clear, starlit night. You can paint the effects of moonlight straight from memory, based on observation, but you cannot paint by moonlight or starlight.

SHADOWS CAST BY THE SUN

The light rays of the sun radiate in every possible direction, but we see only the rays that hit our planet. The sun, however, is so far distanced from Earth, and our planet is so small compared with the sun, that the rays of the sun reaching our globe are parallel as far as we're concerned. This means that the shadows cast by sunlight are all in the same direction on as large a section of Earth as we can possibly see. (Perhaps astronauts, hundreds of miles above Earth, can notice the fact that the shadows are not the same beyond a certain perimeter.) Sunlight moves with the globe. Thus,

if you paint outdoors, especially during seasons when the days are shorter, shadows change considerably within a couple of hours. The light may come from the upper left side in the morning, so that shadows are on the right side of each object. By noon, the sun is almost directly above your head, causing objects to have small shadows only. By mid-afternoon, the light comes from the opposite direction, and shadows are consequently reversed. They also grow longer and longer towards evening as the sun goes lower. If you make the mistake, quite common among art students, of finishing one part of your picture before going to the next part, you may find yourself doing just about the oddest imaginable thing. You will have a painting in which some shadows are on the right, others on the left, and still others in-between. I've seen this happen, especially in cityscapes: Shadows under roofs, eaves, balconies, windowsills were different on every house! The correct procedure is to lay out all shadows and lights at the same time, when you believe they are most satisfactory from an artistic viewpoint. Paint them that way, regardless of the motion of Earth and the continuous changing of the shadows. Or work only for a couple of hours and return to the same place the next day, at the same time, and, naturally, in the same kind of weather. Shadows and lights change according to atmospheric conditions. They are clear and sharp on a sunny day, hazy and indistinct on a cloudy day.

CAFÉ AT VILLEFRANCE-LE-CONFLENT by Diana Armfield
Here the artist has conveyed the effects of light and sunshine by using the pastels very freely, allowing some of the original drawing lines and areas of the paper to show through in places. The picture gives a strong impression of light and life, and conveys the feeling of relaxation associated with an outdoor café on a fine day.

COLOUR MIXING

As well as blending adjacent colours, you can also apply one colour on top of another and blend the two to form a third colour.

For example, by applying strokes of red over strokes of yellow and rubbing them together with your fingertip, a rag or a torchon, you can create an orange, the specific shade depending on the particular red and yellow. You can either blend the colours entirely or only partially to create a broken-colour effect, which appears more vibrant.

The photograph (right) shows some of the different effects that can be created by laying colours on top of one another so that they blend visually. In the first example, light brown has been applied over dark blue-grey; in the second, the same colour combination has been blended with the fingers; while the third uses the same technique as the first but with paler colours—dove grey and beige.

SECONDARY MIXTURES

Cadmium red

Cadmium yellow

The secondary colours – oranges, greens, and purples – are a combination of two primary colours: red + yellow, blue + yellow and red + blue.

Secondaries can be achieved by applying one primary over another, but sometimes this works less well than using a ready-made secondary.

French ultramarine

Cadmium yellow

Crimson lake

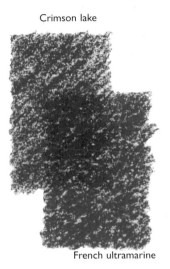

French ultramarine

MIXING COMPLEMENTARY COLOURS

Mixtures made by applying one colour over its complementary, or opposite on the colour wheel, are especially useful for shadows, which often lack sparkle. The mixtures here are half-and-half, but you can also use touches of a complementary colour to grey a hue. If a green in the middle distance of a landscape looks too bright, for example, lay a very light veil of red over it.

Cadmium tangerine

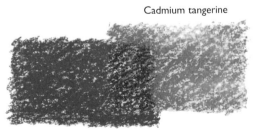

French ultramarine

Hooker's green

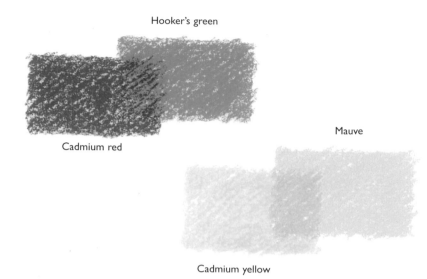

Cadmium red

Mauve

Cadmium yellow

ALTERING COLOURS

Colours can be lightened, darkened, or modified in any number of ways by applying one over another. Yellow over green produces a pale but vivid yellow-green; green over cerulean blue a subtle blue-green; and the same green over ultramarine a stronger blue-green. Lemon yellow over burnt sienna makes a subtle orange; red mixed with burnt umber produces a rich colour more interesting than the umber alone; and ultramarine blue deepens and enriches the green-grey. Conduct some experiments of your own – it is the best way to learn about colour mixing.

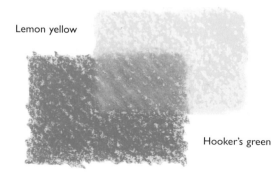

Lemon yellow

Hooker's green

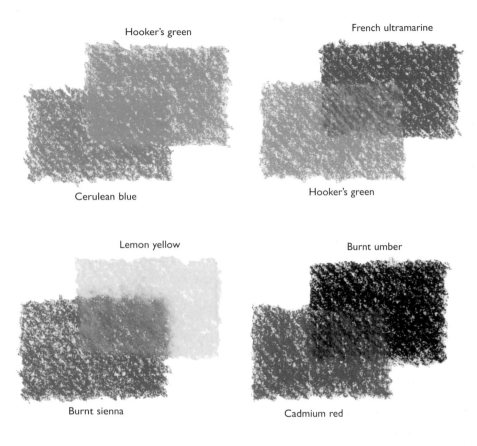

Hooker's green

French ultramarine

Cerulean blue

Hooker's green

Lemon yellow

Burnt umber

Burnt sienna

Cadmium red

Green-grey

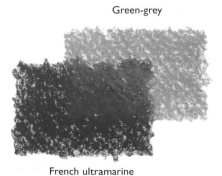

French ultramarine

COLOUR MIXING DEMONSTRATION

The obvious difference between pastels and the moist paint media is that you cannot pre-mix colours. This does not mean that you have to find individual pastel sticks to match every variation in your subject, but you do need to create equivalent values of light and dark tones, brilliant and muted hues. In Hazel Harrison's pastel painting, linear marks and grainy side strokes gradually mix and blend on the paper surface.

1 *The artist chooses to work on a light buff-coloured paper, which gives a softer background for keying the colours than pure white paper. She sketches out the still life loosely with a neutral grey pastel, then starts roughly blocking in areas of local colour; but even at this early stage, she modifies her colours towards the light and dark tones that give form to the objects.*

2 *As the painting progresses, the artist pays attention to accentuating the biases of the hues. She achieves the variety of blues, for example, by selecting shades of cobalt for the right-hand ball of wool, ultramarine at the back, and cerulean and turquoise on the left. However, the dark-toned colours used for shading are less variable and help to unify different parts of the painting.*

3 *The colour interactions are becoming more complex; brownish shading in Indian red gives intensity to the dark pink skein of wool, while the vivid mid-pink is modified with red-violet. These colours are not an exact match for the real colours but create the right balance of hues.*

4 *The weight and texture of the pastel strokes are important aspects of making the colours work effectively. Because pastel is opaque, you can work light over dark and vice versa. Fine linear strokes mesh easily; more emphatic broad strokes heighten the colours and texture.*

5 *Having built up the warm pinks and browns representing the patterned tablecloth and cast shadows, the artist makes a number of finishing touches to adjust the overall tonal balance. Light colours are intensified and offset by subtle shading with cool, mid-toned blues and purples.*

LEARNING FROM THE MASTERS

By studying the drawings and paintings of famous artists, we can recognize the wonderful impulsive style that marks the individual. In the fifteenth century da Vinci was known to colour his drawings with dry pigment, and throughout the centuries many great artists such as Renoir, Degas and Picasso also used pastels. Although you will wish to develop your own style, learning some of the tricks from the Masters is sure to wet your appetite for pastel art.

TURNER

Joseph Mallard William Turner (1775–1851) is recognized today as a genius, perhaps the greatest landscape painter in the entire history of art.

Turner's later works, with their dazzling technical innovations, have provided inspiration for many generations of artists, and continue to do so today, but they failed to please some contemporary critics, who dismissed them with phrases such as 'whitewash and spinach.' In spite of this, Turner had many enlightened patrons and admirers, and was highly successful in his lifetime. His background was humble, but his father, a London barber, was quick to notice his son's talent. He encouraged him to study watercolour, and later became his business manager. Turner's career began as a topographical artist, making accurate and precise drawings of landscapes and architectural subjects. These were later sold to engravers or became the basis for watercolours. He continued to use watercolour and oil hand in hand throughout his life, exhibiting his first oil painting at the Royal Academy in 1796, and continuing to show paintings annually. By the age of 30, he was making a more than adequate income and was able to build his own gallery, where he showed his more controversial works. He died a rich man, leaving a bequest of about 300 paintings and thousands of drawings and paintings to the nation.

NORHAM CASTLE, SUNRISE BY J. M. W. Turner, c. 1835–1840

Norham Castle was a subject that Turner returned to several times over his long career. He had made a watercolour of it in 1797, and this, exhibited at London's Royal Academy, was so successful that he first included it in a book of engravings, and subsequently reworked it as an illustration for a book on English rivers. This later painting, however, is very different from the watercolour, which, like many of his early watercolours, was made with the commercial market in mind. This was painted for his own satisfaction, was never exhibited, and is officially described as unfinished. It dates from a period in Turner's life when he was becoming increasingly fascinated by atmospheric effects in landscape, and experimenting with ways of conveying these in terms of pure colour. The usual oil-painting practice at that time was to work on a mid-toned ochre ground, but Turner abandoned this in favour of white canvas, with the effect of heightening the tones by reflecting back through the thinly applied layers of colour. This use of reflected white is basically a watercolour technique that Turner was able to adopt to oils through his mastery of both media.

How Turner Created This Picture

EQUIVALENT COLOURS
If you were to recreate the colours of the original painting in pastel, these colours would be useful as a basic palette:

POINTS TO WATCH
To create this kind of misty, atmospheric effect, it is essential to give as much thought to tone as you do so colour. When you look at a landscape in bright sunlight, you will see strong dark/light contrasts, but a diffused light like this evens out the tones; a monochrome photograph would record a series of mid-toned greys, with no black or white. Also the edges of any objects will be softer than they are in strong light, and shapes will look flatter, with little detail. There is always a danger that a misty scene may look flat and dull, so don't sacrifice colour to strict authenticity. Instead, follow Turner's example, and use pure colours in a high tonal key.

Sky:

Castle and hills:

Cow and foreground:

FOCUS ON COLOUR
Turner has expressed the quality of the light through the use of a limited range of colours in a high tonal key, that is, with no dark areas. By working with thin veils of semi-transparent colour, he was able to use the white of the canvas as a positive element. The simple, but highly effective, colour scheme is based on the three primary colours:

Controlled tones and colours (left)
This detail shows how skilfully the tones and colours have been controlled, with just a whisper of darker tone separating the hill from the sky, and then the hill from the lines of trees beneath. All the secondary colours contain components of the three primaries; for example, there is a little red in the mixture for the hill, and the sky grades from muted yellow on the left to a warm blue-grey on the right. This gives the painting a complete unity of colour that contributes to the brilliance of the overall effect.

blue, red and yellow. This almost certainly departed from the literal truth; a subject like this would probably have contained little pure colour. Turner was criticized for inventing colour and light effects, but we now appreciate the value of judicious invention, and heightening colours is relatively commonplace.

Colour relationships (left)

In keeping with the misty, atmospheric effect, the red is not used at full strength but is slightly muted, both in tone and in hue. But it appears intense because of its relationship with the surrounding colours – delicate pale-toned mauve-greys and creamy yellows.

Primary contrast (left)

The contrast of colours and tones is strongest in the central area. Blue and yellow are opposites on the colour wheel and always set up vibrant effects. Also, blue is a naturally darker colour than yellow, so there is a built-in element of tonal contrast.

135

Constable

John Constable (1776–1837) was unusual for his time in that he never left his native country.

Not for him the grand splendour of the Alps, sought by many other contemporary painters, including Turner; Constable's enduring love was the English landscape. 'The sound of water escaping from mill dams, willows, old rotten planks . . . I love such things. These scenes made me a painter.'

He was the son of a prosperous mill owner in Suffolk, England, and although he showed an interest in painting from an early age, he did not fully adopt the profession until 1799, when he enrolled as a student at the Royal Academy. His early works were clumsy; realizing their inadequacies, Constable started copying old masters to teach himself technique and composition. Gradually he began to combine lessons learned from past masters with his own observations. Well before 1821, when he painted *The Haywain*, he found his own voice as an artist. In 1816 Constable's father died, leaving him financially secure and thus able to marry Maria Bicknell, whom he had courted for seven years, against the wishes of her family. They were a devoted couple, and he was deeply distressed by her death in 1828, his unhappiness little alleviated by his long-delayed election to the Royal Academy the following year. He had never been held in high regard by the English artistic establishment, and an auction of his paintings held after his death aroused little interest. Most were bought by members of his family.

WEYMOUTH BAY by John Constable, c. 1816

Constable was the first artist to fully realize the importance of skies in the composition of landscape paintings, and to treat them with such truth. Totally committed to the depiction of the English landscape, he was determined to see nature with his own eyes, rather than following a series of recipes laid down by previous masters. His practice was to make small, rapidly executed oil sketches, recording cloud formations and colour effects under different conditions, thus amassing visual reference to be used in his large studio paintings exhibited at the Royal Academy,
such as the well-known Haywain *(he called these his 'six-footers'). Today his spontaneous sketches, showing a direct link with the approach of the Impressionists, are more admired than the 'worked-up' paintings demanded by the taste of the times. This work, demonstrating Constable's free, but assured, technique at its best, with the varied and decisive brushwork giving a strong sense of movement lacking from the studio paintings, was almost certainly painted directly from the subject, though this is not known for certain.*

How Constable Created This Picture

EQIVALENT COLOURS

If you were to try to recreate the colours of the original painting in pastel, the colours in the charts to the right would be useful as a basic palette.

POINTS TO WATCH

One of the pitfalls in landscape painting is a failure to relate the sky to the land in terms of colour. By working on a coloured ground, and deliberately leaving parts of it uncovered in both areas of the painting, you will achieve a unity of colour that will help the painting to hang together as a whole. Always look for ways of setting up these colour echoes, perhaps introducing touches of the land colour into the sky, and vice versa. Make sure also that your technique is consistent throughout the picture, and avoid treating one area in a tighter, more detailed manner than another.

FOCUS ON TECHNIQUE

If you compare a photograph of a sky-dominated landscape with a painting such as this, or an Impressionist work, you can appreciate the importance of the artist's craft immediately. Photographs freeze the subject, making clouds appear solid and static, but as you can see from this painting, an artist is able to suggest the movement of the sky and the way the clouds are constantly forming and re-forming by the way he or she uses brushstrokes. You can do very much the same thing in pastel by varying the direction and weight of the strokes and using a sharp edge to

Sky:

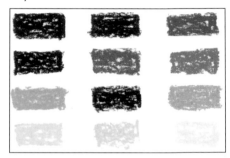

Sea and landscape:

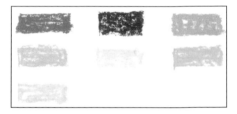

Foliage:

add occasional touches of crisp definition. You can also avoid the risk of overworking by using the paper as a colour in its own right, as Constable has done here.

Moving water (right)

As with skies, using a tight, over-controlled technique for moving water can destroy the feeling of movement, so take care not to overwork it. Constable has employed the same shorthand method as for the clouds, painting the sea with just a few long strokes crossing one another in places, and leaving much of the ground colour showing. Gently curving strokes, made with thicker paint, follow the direction of the wave breaking on and drawing back from the sand, employing the movement.

Brushwork (left)

The variety of the brushwork is especially noticeable in this area, with some strokes curving around the cloud shapes, and others running in straight diagonals and counter-diagonals. The darker tones have been worked wet into wet over lighter colours so that the boundaries between tones are soft and blurred. For crisper effects, such as the edges where the white cloud on the right meets the blue sky, the paint has been used more thickly, the equivalent of a heavily applied pastel stroke.

Ground colour (left)

When painting on the spot, time is always a factor, and working on a coloured ground cuts down painting time, because parts of it can be left alone, with no added colour. Here, the ground has been left uncovered to represent the whole of the beach, with just a few light strokes and dabs of paint laid over it in strategic places. The stones in the immediate foreground are painted firmly, again with directional brushstrokes and strong tonal contrasts that bring the area forward in space.

Vincent van Gogh

Vincent van Gogh (1853–1890) has become an almost legendary figure – the epitome of the struggling artist who failed dismally during his lifetime, yet whose works now command record prices.

Had he lived for a normal lifespan, van Gogh probably would have achieved some degree of fame and financial reward, because by the time of his tragically early death his unique and extraordinary talent was beginning to be recognized by other artists.

Van Gogh did not begin to paint until 1880, after several false starts in life. First he worked for his uncle, an art dealer, in London and Paris, and then he became an unpaid schoolteacher in England before deciding on a vocation as a lay preacher – his father was a Protestant pastor. It was during two years spent as a preacher in a grim, impoverished mining district of Belgium that his religious zeal channelled itself into his true vocation, and he decided to become an artist. He was supported by his loyal and generous brother, Theo, who gave him an allowance from his own small salary, and for the ten years that remained of his life he painted with single-minded passion, even during his spells in the lunatic asylum. He had his first mental breakdown in 1888, just a month after completing the painting featured here, and shot himself less than two years later. It is a sad irony that he failed even in his last act, missing his heart, and dying in his bed in the village of Auvers, with his grief-stricken brother by his side.

VINCENT'S CHAIR WITH HIS PIPE by Vincent van Gogh, 1888

The label 'still life' creates a mental picture of objects on a table top, and indeed, the majority of still lifes do feature fruit, flowers, bottles and so on, arranged on a surface roughly corresponding to the artist's eye level. But any painting of inanimate objects can be described as still life. Van Gogh is not just painting a chair; he is painting his own chair in the house in Arles where he lived for a time, stamping his personality on it by including the pipe he smoked when relaxing. The picture, together with another he painted of the bedroom of the house, tells a story about his life at the time. Van Gogh frequently painted personal possessions in this way; for example, one still life shows a pile of books, and another a pair of battered boots.

Another departure from the more usual still-life set-up is the choice of a high viewpoint; he is looking down on the chair from above, so that the rush seat is seen in its entirety and the chair fills the whole of the central area of the picture.

How van Gogh Created This Picture

EQUIVALENT COLOURS

If you were to try to recreate the colours of the original painting in pastel, the following colours would be useful as a basic palette:

Background:

Pipe and rag:

Box:

Floor:

Chair:

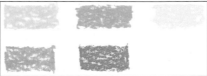

POINTS TO WATCH

When painting a single object, such as this chair, plan the composition with as much care for the other elements as for the object itself. But remember that the object will be the focal point, so first decide how you will place it on the rectangle of your picture surface, whether to crop part of it or show it complete, and what viewpoint you will choose. If you want to paint the kind of semi-autobiographical still life that van Gogh has, consider introducing some personal possession that you are fond of or that helps to explain your interests. A sketchbook, a jar of paintbrushes, or a bag of knitting wools could be the equivalent of van Gogh's pipe. Finally, when you start to paint, try to give the subject extra interest by the way you handle the medium. In pastel you cannot emulate van Gogh's luscious, thick paint, but you can add an extra dimension by using varied strokes.

Red/green contrasts (right)

This passage of the painting brings in muted versions of the other pair of complementary colours, red and green, with mixtures made from these two colours. Notice how the richest area of red, behind the strut of the chair, is balanced by a slash of green, while the other tiles are painted with interweaving brushstrokes of greens, reds and pinks.

Colour and tone (above left)

Here, you can see the juxtaposition of one pair of complementary colours, blue and orange-yellow. These contrasts work best if the colours are kept close in tone, as they are here, with the blue mixed with white to equal the naturally lighter tone of the yellow. The colour theme is repeated on the door, with a thin stripe of yellow painted over the blue wet into wet, so that the two colours have mixed slightly.

Structural emphasis (above right)

The bold blue outlines around the legs and struts of the chair give strength and solidity to the structure, as well as continuing the complementary colour theme and separating the blue and yellow areas from the red and green areas of the floor.

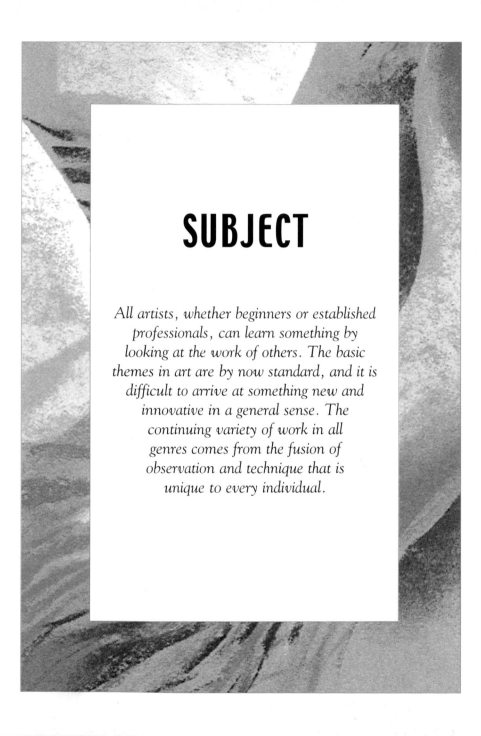

SUBJECT

All artists, whether beginners or established professionals, can learn something by looking at the work of others. The basic themes in art are by now standard, and it is difficult to arrive at something new and innovative in a general sense. The continuing variety of work in all genres comes from the fusion of observation and technique that is unique to every individual.

STILL LIFE

The great advantage of still life is that you can choose a subject entirely within your control. Unlike a person or animal, it doesn't walk away; unlike landscape subjects, it does not bend with the breeze or change character when the sun goes down. You can use a still life for a period of extended study, resulting in just one pastel rendering or many, so it is an excellent vehicle for learning your craft and sharpening your powers of observation.

SUBJECTS

Natural objects readily present themselves as elements of still life because they have distinctive forms and varied colours and textures that give you plenty to work on at a relatively small scale. Flowers, fruits and vegetables are the most obvious and perhaps most commonly chosen candidates. For the same reasons, domestic objects with reflective or patterned surfaces, such as bowls, jugs, pans and bottles made of metal, ceramic or glass are favourite components of still life. Often fabric is introduced, such as a tablecloth or curtain, to give a soft contrast to solid forms.

Less obvious but equally promising subjects can be found randomly anywhere around the home – clothes and shoes, furniture, cushions and rugs, books and ornaments, garden tools, or brushes and pencils stored in jars in your studio. Any of these objects can be deliberately arranged, or you can treat them as 'found groupings' and just study them as they are.

VARIATIONS

The scale of such still lifes lends itself to pastel work, but you need not be restricted to the domestic context. Different but equally 'still' subjects come from the absence of human activity in normally busy scenes – empty deck chairs by the riverside or seafront, small boats tied to a dock, machinery on a building site standing idle outside working hours. There are also natural and man-made features in the landscape that provide outdoor still life constructions – rocks and stones, for instance, or fences, walls and gateways. Such subjects incorporate many interesting elements of shape, form, colour and texture.

Whether you are drawing one object or many, and whatever scale you are working to, the active qualities of the marks you make with pastel can contribute a special character to the rendering. Be prepared to experiment with technique and try out alternative solutions. Even a simple arrangement of two or three fruits can be interpreted in a variety of ways.

REFLECTIONS
by Sandra Burshell

This group was essentially happened upon and adjusted to improve the composition. There is, however, a carefully planned colour theme based on the contrast between warm red-browns and turquoise-blue walls. The artist muted and 'blued' the green of the plant so that it does not conflict with this theme.

Choosing the Group

A still life usually has a theme, giving the impression that the objects belong naturally together. In a found group a theme will already exist, but in a deliberate arrangement you will need to select items that combine comfortably.

A popular still life theme is the culinary one — a group of fruits, vegetables, or other food, perhaps combined with dishes, cutlery or kitchen utensils. Texture can also be a theme, with components such as glass, metal and fabrics selected for their surface qualities. Or you could make colour the main theme, choosing a collection of blue objects but including a yellow or red one for contrast. Contrast is always important in painting, so avoid items that are all the same shape or colour to get an interesting result. If you decide to paint a bowl of fruit, for example, see if you can introduce something angular as a counterpoint to the rounded shapes. This linear touch could be provided by the back and front of the tabletop, or you could include a book or napkin.

EXPLORING ARRANGEMENTS

You should avoid introducing too many colours because they will tend to cancel one another out and the painting will lack coherence. Have some contrasts, though, of colour and shape; in all these arrangements the oranges and yellows offset the deep blues, and the tall bottles make a good background for the predominant circles and curves. When setting out a still life, it is a good idea to start with more objects than you think you will need and gradually eliminate items as you try out different arrangements.

Over-cluttered, and glass bottle colour insufficiently strong. Jug facing outwards draws eye out of picture. Pattern on ginger jar fights tablecloth.

ARRANGING THE GROUP

Artists who specialize in still life spend a considerable time setting up their groups, and you must be prepared to do the same. This is the first step towards composing the picture. There are no definite rules about arrangement, but bear in mind that even an organized group should look as natural as possible. Also, you need to establish spatial relationships that tie the different elements together visually.

Once you have made a preliminary choice of objects, assemble them, then move them around until the group coheres.

If the composition looks cluttered, edit your original choice. Novices tend to overcrowd their still lifes. Let certain objects overlap, and position some nearer the back of the table than others. Watch out for spaces between them; if one component is too far from another, it will become isolated and destroy the group relationship.

When you begin to feel that the arrangement is working, look at it through a viewfinder to check whether it will fit properly into your picture area. If it doesn't, make some final adjustments until you are happy with the appearance of the group.

Much better. The jug now takes the eye in. Fruit in foreground balances that in bowl, and folds of tablecloth give movement.

White cloth shows up colours and creates attractive blue shadows from glass. Could be toned down in painting to avoid stark contrast.

Composing the Painting

You may think that you have completed the composition once you have arranged the group, but this is only the beginning. Before you start to paint, you must work out what viewpoint to take, what shape the painting is to be, and how you will place the subject on the paper.

The viewfinder is helpful again here. You may find that it reveals possibilities you have not previously considered, such as observing the group from above or below.

A high viewpoint, such as you have when you work standing up, is often effective for an arrangement that includes dishes or bowls because it allows you to see more of the circles, introducing a pattern element. A low viewpoint from a seated position can work well for a group of tall objects, such as bottles.

If your still life is on a table-top, try looking at it from one side so that you see the corner of the table, rather than head on, which gives you a hard horizontal line in the foreground. It is usually best to avoid horizontals, as they block the eye rather than leading it into the picture, creating a static effect. A device often adopted to break the line of the table edge is a piece of drapery hanging over the front and sweeping around the objects, making a series of curves and diagonal lines from foreground to background.

CHOOSING VIEWPOINT

You can spend time arranging a still life only to find that it loses its appeal when you return to your easel. This is because you have shifted your viewpoint, which radically changes the visual relationship of the objects. So before you begin to paint, look at the group through a viewfinder from your painting position, and if it still does not gel, move your easel, or work from a standing position so that you can look down on the subject.

High viewpoint (standing position). Most suitable for flat objects, and works well for dishes and fruit. But foreshortening of bottle and jar looks uncomfortable.

Eye-level viewpoint is good, stressing diagonal side of bowl, tall glass bottle, and upward-sweeping folds of drapery. Also creates an oval ellipse of the plate in the foreground.

Viewing from left makes drapery into interesting shape and causes bowl to overlap brown jar. Gives a pleasing impression of movement.

FRUIT STILL LIFE by Catherine Nicodemo
A strong pattern derives partly from the way the fruit is arranged and partly from the high viewpoint. This enhances shapes because forms are less apparent, and it separates the objects from the flat plane on which they are resting. The artist emphasized the separation by omitting any shadows beneath the fruit, so that they look as though they are flying upwards.

Fruit

The great variety of fruit gives you a choice of many different qualities of form, colour and texture.

You can focus on the sculptural elements of volume and contour, modelling the forms with subtle gradations of light and shade, or you can emphasize the colours and textures, working the pastel marks into an almost abstract pattern that incorporates all the variations of surface detail.

Depending on your approach, you may want to isolate the subject and treat it as a self-contained form, or you may prefer to give it a context that includes other objects and a recognizable background. When you are working with simple forms, the quality of light is important. Angled light will emphasize the structure of the object, whereas an even spread of light may flatten the forms and reduce the range of visual interest.

LEMONS by Sally Strand

The simple shapes in this composition are a strong vehicle for the artist's exceptional skill as a colourist. Each of the lemons is modelled with a range of subtle hues, from warm yellow and pink to cold blue, green and lilac. The effect of brilliant sunlight derives from bold definition of the highlight areas.

BOWL OF CHERRIES (Conté oil pastels and pastel pencils on watercolour paper)

This bold, bright still life is a good example of working with a limited palette; the artist has used only a few colours but has managed to make them say a good deal. Art teachers are fond of giving their pupils such exercises as using only the three primaries or no more than four colours, and these can provide an excellent discipline; by limiting your colour range you are forced to make decisions about composition or the placing of lights and darks which you might otherwise contrive to avoid.

The composition here is based on the juxtaposition of the reds and blues, with the two cherries on the table balancing those in the bowl. The reds, because they are warmer than the blue, assume more importance, but since the blue itself is a relatively warm one, the whole picture has a bright, cheerful look suitable to the subject.

1 *There are lots of strong colours used here. To keep them from looking too flat, the artist has started to build up areas like the cherries. Here she is working on the bowl. First she outlines it lightly in blue, and then she moves to the shadow area.*

2 *The green leaf could end up looking lost among so much intense colouring, so the artist is sharpening it up by etching in the veins with a knife, a technique called sgraffito.*

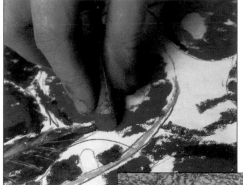

3 This detail shows the range of reds, pinks and purples the artist has used to build up the fruit, with the darker colours used to model them by suggesting the shadows.

4 I like the way the turquoise helps define the fruit bowl so that the cherries don't dominate too much, and the artist has pulled the ultramarine away from the concentrated block of shadow to suggest the reflection from the window. It also gives unity to the picture; but because it's a cooler colour than the red of the cherries, it does not vie for attention.

Patterns

Many still life groupings provide a wealth of pattern elements, both in the juxtaposition of varied shapes and forms and in the flat patterns often used to decorate domestic items such as containers, ornaments and upholstery.

Because you can treat pastel as a medium of line or of mass, it is particularly well suited to pattern-making. Distinct pattern elements can be drawn with the pastel stick, using outlines and linear marks to describe individual shapes and surface details. Colour areas can be laid in as solidly shaded, blended, or broken colour. Use the mark-making capabilities of the pastel to match specific elements of your subject.

Imposed patterns, such as glazed decoration on ceramic ware or printed fabric patterns, are designed to create a colourful surface effect, an element that adds liveliness to your rendering. In a still life, however, they are not seen plainly as flat patterns but as an additional element of form. You may notice how the imposed pattern can describe something about the underlying structure of the patterned object or material – distortion of the pattern as it wraps around a bowl or jug, for instance, or breaks in continuity that signify fabric folds.

PAINTING PATTERNS

Doortop ornaments, lampshade and door knob clutter and weaken the composition. Door knob changed to white in painting.

Door mouldings, hardly visible in the photograph, need to be enhanced to make the background less starkly white.

A dark shadow under the table separates the tablecloth from the rug. Artist lengthened the tablecloth and reduced the shadow to link the two areas.

INTERIOR WITH PATTERNED CARPET by Pip Carpenter

As you can see if you compare the photograph from the previous page with the painting, judicious selection and rejection created a stronger composition. The most important change was to tilt the perspective to show more of the table-top and rug. The doors and the vertical edge of the wall on the right now provide a good balance for the wall hanging.

Groups

There are two main schools of still life painters: those who set up elaborate arrangements containing many objects and those who prefer simple groups.

The Dutch painters of the 17th and 18th centuries, who established still life as a painting subject, belonged to the first category. The French

Impressionists, concerned with being true to what they saw, chose humble subjects, such as a plate, knife and loaf of bread on a table. Both approaches are valid, but if you want to follow the Dutch example, you will need a good selection of objects, so start collecting suitable fabrics, china and glassware.

YELLOW CABINET WITH CUPS AND SAUCERS by Deborah Deichler
These two paintings differ in lighting and technique as well as in subject matter. Hard front lighting, casting the minimum of shadow, illuminates each object, which the artist drew in minute detail. She began with pastel pencils and hard pastels, then combined these with soft pastels to build up smoothly blended surfaces in which no pastel marks are visible.

THE BLUE VASE by Margaret Glass
In contrast to the deliberate arrangement above, these objects seem to belong on the windowsill, and the technique is much freer. The primary theme of the picture is light, which comes from behind the group so that the shadows play a vital role in the composition. Both the window and the framed photograph are suggested rather than portrayed literally, to prevent them from dominating the picture.

FOLIAGE AND FLOWERS

The immense amount of detail contained within any landscape view can be focused more closely in individual studies of foliage and flowers. This is an opportunity to experiment technically, and find out how the different kinds of pastel marks convey the extraordinary range of natural leaf and flower forms.

Because the shapes, textures and colour nuances in landscape are so complex, it is often tempting to settle for a broadly impressionistic style that creates a striking image but glosses over the characteristic detail of individual elements. In choosing a particular feature of landscape for more intense study, you can deal with the smaller subtleties of form and colour, acquiring information that will feed back into your broader landscape views.

Even when you limit yourself to an individual subject of this kind, there are still many different aspects to it, and your representation need not be comprehensive or realistic. Look for the essential details and qualities that enable you to produce a convincing account of your own visual impression.

A POT OF GERANIUMS AND FUCHSIAS
by Maureen Jordan
The artist has focused on the group of flowers in their blue tub. But the garden setting has given her the opportunity to exploit both the pattern of leaves and the texture of the foreground flagstones.

IRISES
by Anthony Eyton
The mass of foliage is freely translated with gestural drawing, but confident handling of the complex structure and varied colour range produces a striking description.

CHERRY TREE IN BLOSSOM
by Geoff Marsters
A consistent pattern of small, hooked linear marks describes variations of texture and local colour, relying on the balance of colour to define form.

159

Arranging an Indoor Group

Arranging flowers for a painting differs from making a floral display.

In general, it is best to aim for simplicity and a natural look rather than the formal, symmetrical florists' style, which can appear static in a painting. Let some of the flowers droop over the edge of the vase, and do not have all the blooms facing forward as though they were posing for a photograph. You will have a greater variety of shapes if some are turned away.

Do not overdo contrasts of colour. The most successful flower paintings either have one dominant hue, with perhaps a touch of complementary colour for contrast (say, a bunch of blue flowers with one small orange one), or a range of harmonizing colours, such as blues, mauves and pinks. Too many colours will make the picture look disjointed and jumpy.

When you have arranged the flowers, look through a viewfinder and see if the composition needs improvement. You may notice that you have a lot of blank space in the front of the picture beside the vase. This can happen with groups that make too tall a shape to fill the standard rectangular paper format. You can solve the problem by introducing another element beside the vase, such as a glass, bowl, or one or two pieces of fruit. An even simpler solution is to break off one of the blooms and place it by the vase, or to wait until some petals have dropped and leave them there, which looks completely natural.

ZINNIAS IN VASE by Maria Pinschof
To capture flowers, it can help to work in colour immediately, without making a preliminary drawing, as was done here. The artist vitalized the picture by building it up in a series of lines flowing in the direction of the vase and flowers, and using scribbles in foreground and background.

SETTING UP A FLORAL GROUP

You can make a striking painting out of a very simple subject, such as a bunch of wild flowers in a jar or one rose in a small bowl, but if you decide on a mixed group, take some time over arranging it, as this is the first step in composing your picture. Try to achieve a harmony of colours, or restrict yourself to one or two colours, and try out several different vases to see which one sets off the flowers best. The photographs here will give you some ideas.

Complementary colours – yellow and violet – have been used to striking effect in this group. It is cleverly arranged, with the spray of foliage making a sweeping curve that breaks up the top edge of the vase and adds foreground interest.

This arrangement of white lilies has strength and simplicity, and the straight-sided vase is a good choice. To paint it, you might need to introduce some colour variation into the background to prevent it from looking dull.

This is a nicely balanced, natural-looking arrangement, with the squat, heavy-glass vase complementing the flowers well and contrasting with the round table.

SIMPLIFYING FLOWER SHAPES

When you first look at a multi-petalled flower, such as a dahlia or chrysanthemum, it seems complex, with many different planes and surfaces. But there are basic shapes in flowers: Most are circles, bell shapes or cones. Some are a combination; the daffodil, for example, is a bell shape set in a circle. Try to identify these shapes, and notice how they are affected by perspective. A sunflower (circle) seen at an angle becomes an ellipse, and if you draw this accurately you will have no trouble placing the petals around it.

The trumpet of a daffodil is bell-shaped, but from the front you will still see two circles: the nearest edge of the trumpet and the halo of surrounding petals.

A sunflower seen from the front forms two circles, an inner one for the centre of the flower and an outer one for the petals. Sometimes there will be more than one layer of petals.

Viewed from a three-quarter angle, the central circle becomes an ellipse and may hide some or all of the petals on the far side.

From a side or three-quarter view, the bell shape can be seen clearly, and the halo of outer petals forms an ellipse.

Painting Flowers Outdoors

Painting flowers out-of-doors presents you with a wide range of choices and thus many decisions that have to be made.

Any painting, of course, involves decision-making. When you are dealing with an indoor set-up or a close-up study, for example, you will have to consider colour and composition, but when you take your paints out into the wider world you will be faced with the more difficult decision of what to focus on. Confronted with a field of sunflowers or poppies, or massed flowers in a garden bed, will you single out one plant for close attention or treat the flowers as landscape features, dealing with them in more general terms?

DIFFERENT APPROACHES

Your choices will depend partly on your own interests and partly on the flowers. Many wild flowers, such as bluebells and primroses, grow in masses, and this is part of their charm. Others, such as the foxglove or the dramatic tall plants of the Umbelliferae family, could make a lovely study on their own, set against their natural background. In a small patio garden, flowers and plants in tubs could be treated in much the same way as an indoor flower arrangement, with the bonus of allowing you to exploit the effects of sunlight and shadow. In a large garden, perhaps that of a public park, the overall colour scheme of an individual bed could provide inspiration for your painting, and you could treat the flowers in a more generalized way. If you observe the shapes, colour and growth habit carefully, you will find that you can suggest a particular flower quite accurately with a few well-placed brushstrokes or pastel marks without going into detail.

COMPOSITION

If you decide on a broad view, you must think about the composition and focal point, and consider what you might leave out or play down. A viewfinder is a great help in the planning stages of a painting, so ensure that this is part of your equipment. Do not be afraid to rearrange nature in the interests of your painting. Artistic licence is more than just a figure of speech, and you can move a bush from one place to another or leave it out altogether if you wish. You can also exaggerate some feature in your subject, perhaps giving more emphasis to the shapes and colours of shadows in the foreground or on pathways. If you make shadows part of the composition, paint them first, or at least make a note of their direction, as they will change dramatically as the day progresses.

If you choose to focus closely on one or two plants, avoid letting the background become too dominant or it will detract from the focal point. Often you can treat background flowers, foliage or trees as nebulous shapes or simply areas of colour. This will also help you create the sense of space that an outdoor subject demands.

Portrait format

Landscape format

COMPOSITION OUT-OF-DOORS

Decide what to leave out and the composition will begin to take shape. A viewfinder is a great aid, though making a square with your first fingers and thumbs is almost as good. A homemade viewfinder is made of two L-shaped pieces of cardboard joined together with paper clips.

ASTERS: SOFT PASTEL

Small multi-headed flowers like these look best as a massed group; making a study of an individual flower would be good practice, but it would lack impact as a painting. The artist has chosen soft pastel, an ideal choice, as it allows him to make expressive lines as well as building up rich colours. When working in this medium, remember that you can mix and blend colours simply by laying one over another. You can also rub colours together with your fingers for soft effects, but too much of this kind of blending can produce a dull and bland result.

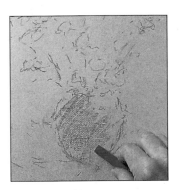

1 *Never make a preliminary drawing for pastel with pencil because it repels the soft colour. You can use charcoal or pastels.*

2 *A little colour has been applied to the background, using the side of a short length of pastel. The artist now sketches in the flowers and stems using the edge of the pastel tip.*

3 *Here a blending tool called a torchon is employed to spread the colour, filling in the gaps between strokes.*

4 *For the area of shadow behind the vase, several colours have been laid down adjacent to and over one another, and a finger is used to blend them.*

165

5 *There is now quite a thick build-up of colour, which has filled the grain of the paper. This makes it difficult to lay more colours on top unless the work is first sprayed with fixative.*

6 *Because the pastel has been fixed, further colour can be applied to the vase. Black is used to increase the depth of shadow beneath the overhanging flower head.*

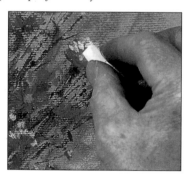

7 *Small details, highlights and colour accents should be left until last or there will be a danger of accidental smudging. The side of the pastel tip is used to make linear white highlights.*

8 *Although some of the background flowers are merely suggested with directional lines of colour, the portrayal is convincing and accurate, and the varied pastel marks create a lively impression in keeping with the subject.*

GERBERA: OIL PASTEL

1 *This bold, simply shaped flower calls for an equally bold treatment; oil pastels are a good choice. Block in the shape, using two or three different shades of red and pink, and letting the pastel marks follow the direction of the petals outwards from the centre.*

2 *Remember that not all the petals are on the same plane. Some are in front of others, forming cast shadows on those behind, so begin to build up the lights and darks. For the flower centre, try a technique called sgraffito, which involves laying two or three colours on top of one another and then scratching into the top layer with a blade.*

3 *Lighten the nearest petals further, then use a dark colour and finer lines to show the way the petals narrow as they gather in at the centre. To suggest the texture of the short, massed stamens, lay more colour in the centre and scratch away again.*

Trees

Trees can either be viewed as part of the general population of a landscape or as special features for close study.

Trees have a fascinating amount of variation in their natural shapes, textures and colours, depending on the characteristics of the individual species and the seasonal changes they undergo.

Although botanical identification is not an essential feature of tree studies, it is important to pay attention to specific visual qualities such as typical outline, branch structure, leaf shape and colour. The more you analyze the particular qualities, the more you can develop the richness and detail of a tree portrait or give definition and contrast to a study of grouped trees.

ASPENS ALONG THE PATH IN THE ROCKIES by Diana Armfield
This image conveys very precisely the detail and character of the slender aspens, and demonstrates how the build-up of many small pastel strokes constructs the impression of form. The soft pastel is handled loosely and economically, blocking in areas of grainy colour and developing textural detail with a variety of linear marks.

AUTUMN TREE by Sally Stride
Using a tree in a landscape view gives an immediate sense of scale. The curving branches lead the eye into the space of the landscape. A free, gestural approach is applied to form and texture, the arrangement of colours helping to define the different elements of the composition.

CREATING DRAMA

CYPRESS
by Kitty Wallis
Here the viewpoint is low. The artist looks up at the trees, which seem to explode into the sky like fireworks. The drama was increased by setting the dark triangle of trees and hill against a pale but glowing sky that occupies a large part of the picture space. Notice how the sky colour is repeated on the tree trunks and branches, illuminated by the sun at top left.

FOREGROUND SHADOWS

SUMMER MORNING
by Alan Oliver
Shadows can play a vital role in composition; they often provide that essential touch of foreground interest, as they do here.
Foreground shadow must not become too dominant, however. The artist worked lightly, leaving patches of bare paper between strokes of dark green to achieve a lively colour mix.

LIGHT AND WEATHER

Inevitably, when you work in colour and are dealing with the theme of landscape, you must focus on the effects of natural light.

LAKE VIEW AT GRAND TETON NATIONAL PARK by Steven Bewsher

In some cases, natural light will be the very essence of your subject. For instance, the charm of a particular view will stem mainly from such effects as dappled light under trees or the warm colours of afternoon light giving extra intensity to the landscape hues.

It can be hard to fix such transient effects when you are working on the spot, and photographs are not always good references as they may lose the colour clarity. Effective interpretation of light qualities comes in large measure from keen observation, but an equally important factor is confidence with your medium. Sometimes it helps to exaggerate contrasts of colour and tone and be bold and free in your mark-making. When you step back from the

drawing, the individual elements magically cohere into a striking image.

A coloured ground is a useful starting point if you are trying to capture brilliant qualities of light. A base colour allows pale tints to stand out fully, whereas when you use white paper its own brilliance is constantly competing with the colours that you apply. Mid-tones and muted hues are probably most suitable for use by beginners, but you can get excellent results using very dark-toned paper.

ATMOSPHERIC LANDSCAPE

Pastel is the perfect medium for gentle, misty light effects. The only possible danger is that you may overblend to produce light tones and gentle gradations, or lose sight of colour altogether and produce a picture in shades of pale grey. In 'Lake View at Grand Teton National Park', Steven Bewsher takes a leaf out of Turner's book and works with vibrant colours in a range running from light to mid-tone. Although he blends colours in the early stages, the blends are overlaid with firm pastel strokes that give the painting an additional surface interest that, in turn, enhances the subject matter.

SUTHERLAND COAST by Aubrey Phillips
Pastel is a marvellous medium for capturing the fleeting effects of light outdoors because it is so quick and responsive. Here the artist has allowed the colour of the paper to establish the overall tonality of the scene. Quick, calligraphic strokes and blendings give an impression of a blustery day.

STUDY OF SUNSET by Doug Dawson
Backlight is moody and atmospheric, creating a sense of mystery and stillness, as in the picture on the left. Sometimes the light catches the edges of objects, producing a lovely halo of light; you can see this on the backs of the cows in this pastoral scene. To capture the effect of backlighting, work mainly within a narrow range of mid-to-dark tones, keep colours cool and muted, downplay details, and brighten the edges of forms where appropriate to indicate the way light glances off them.

Seasons

Each season of the year has its own characteristics, but since you cannot compare them at the same time, a clear sense of seasonal atmosphere comes from careful observation of actual qualities of light, colour and landscape structure.

Autumn is a favoured time for colour studies; the colours of the trees can be sensational in themselves, and are often enhanced by a rich, warm light. Winter is a less inviting time to work outdoors, either drawing or observing the landscape, but it has its particular visual excitement in the skeletal forms of plants and the strange colour range of lights and shadows on snow. The versatility of pastels makes them equally appropriate for emphasizing the calligraphic qualities of winter landscape or expressing the dense massing of colour, light and shade.

Seasonal character can also incorporate a mood, often relating to weather conditions. Landscape rarely appears bleak under brilliant summer sunshine, but heavy storm clouds can make gentle pastoral land seem suddenly threatening.

FARM TRACK IN TUSCANY by David Napp
The technique in this soft pastel painting is very consistent, using short, broad strokes to mix and overlay small patches of colour that gradually coalesce into distinctive shapes and forms. The selection of colours evokes gentle warmth in the landscape, but the sky remains cool, again suggesting a spring-like mood.

AUTUMN NEAR THE ARTIST'S STUDIO by John Elliot

In pastel work it is often advisable to give full rein to the intensity of colour, especially when the technique is free and bold. Oil pastel is used here to develop an active network of linear marks, where strong contrasts of colour and tonal values allow the form and texture of foliage to emerge. A dark, heavily textured ground contributes to the broken colour effects, although in places the pronounced grain of the paper is concealed by thick impasto dashes and streaks of colour.

FROST AT FLATFORD by Margaret Glass
In this frosty scene, pale, delicate tones of colour – pinks, blues and yellows – are superimposed over a warm, mid-tone tinted paper, which can be seen in tiny patches through the broken pastel strokes at all stages along the river.

THE WHITE RIVER by Neil Drevitson
The emphasis is on icy-cold blues reflected in the river and found in the shadows cast on the snow.

Skies

The most problematic aspect of painting skies is that the sky itself is largely composed of light, which you must translate into the colour equivalents provided by a solid, material medium.

How you deal with this in terms of technique depends partly on the overall style of your image. Sky composed of many individual marks building up into a complex feathered texture or mass of broken colour can be surprisingly effective; but if the sky becomes much busier than the landscape, it will begin to dominate the image and destroy the sense of space.

On the other hand, an evenly coloured, open sky may look too flat if treated over-simply. It might be advisable to use two or three closely related tints to give a little depth and variation, blending these if necessary to create a subtly coherent surface effect. Alternatively, you may wish to play up hints of colour or atmosphere, even giving the sky an unnatural colouring that expresses the mood of the image and forms an appropriate backdrop to the landscape subject.

WHEAL BETSY, DARTMOOR by Lionel Aggett
Pastel is a sympathetic medium for describing cloud formations, its softness contributing to the atmospheric elements and its range of luminous hues suited to capturing the varied qualities of natural light. The technique of using broken colour enables the artist to deal with transient light effects.

TOWARDS ARDNAMURCHAN by Geoff Marsters

The flat plane of the sea is often less interesting than the sky, so it makes sense to place the horizon low, letting the sky dominate. Here it occupies two-thirds of the picture space. The artist built up the glowing colours with layer upon layer of pastel in downward strokes, which suggest the weather conditions – showers alternating with sunshine.

LT229, IH88, IH265 AT ALDEBURGH by Geoff Marsters
The colour nuances of a subdued, greying sky are developed with feathering of broad vertical strokes creating gentle gradations of the delicately varied tints.

177

Seascapes

Many artists have gazed at the great formations and colours of clouds and wished they could capture them in pastel. The trouble is that clouds are always on the move, which means you have to work fast. It is an idea to follow the examples of this artist, and work from sketches and photographs.

1 *Working on a warm brown-ochre sandpaper, the artist began with sketchy pastel lines and now works on the sky. This deep blue is the dominant colour, and once it is in place she will be able to assess the colours for the land.*

2 *The artist indicated the full range of colours and tones in the sky before working on the foreground. She needs strong tones to balance those of the clouds, and uses brown, orange and now grey, making firm marks.*

3 *Colour echoes are already being set up: the blue of the sky appears also in the foreground, and some of the browns and ochres of the land are repeated in the clouds.*

4 *You cannot be tentative when working on this kind of paper. The artist makes bold dabs, squiggles and inventive marks in a variety of colours. This area of the picture needs to stand out strongly in order to balance the sky.*

5 *The clouds are softened by applying one colour over another. This method mixes the colours to produce a blended effect but does not remove pigment.*

6 *Sandpaper grips the pigment firmly, but surface dust is removed with a dry, stiff-haired paintbrush. Brushing is needed because too much colour was built up to work over and the artist wants to lay a solid area of white on the cloud top.*

7 *The colours of the sky on a distant horizon are subtle and can be tricky to handle. The artist uses a mixture of colours: a cool blue-green with a warm mauve-blue on top. The first colour comes through slightly, creating a three-dimensional effect.*

8 *The final touch – the figure – is drawn delicately with the pastel tip. This had to be left until last, since it would have been impossible to work around it. Tiny flecks of white, suggesting a collar, link the figure with the white edges of the waves.*

Storms and Rain

*Some of the most atmospheric and dramatic effects of light occur just before,
during, or immediately after a downpour of rain. It is possible to represent
rain itself in a graphic or symbolic manner by manipulating the paint.*

It is often more appropriate to paint not the rain itself but some of the effects it can have. For instance, moisture in the air has a flattening effect on forms, and the effects of aerial perspective are evident over suprisingly short distances. The approach of a storm, of course, offers great potential for dramatic effects. Suggest the brooding, threatening atmosphere by painting the land and upper part of the sky with dark tones, leaving a strip of pale sky near the horizon.

THE YELLOW HOUSE by Jane Strother

A stormy sky creates a threatening mood, its colour and texture giving weight to the image. The atmosphere is underlined by the apparent isolation of the house, centralized within the composition, with the sunlit colours of the house and foreground creating an element of contrast.

Sunlight

A landscape is more than just trees, fields and hills – you must also take account of the prevailing light, because it dictates the colours and tones. The difference between a sunny and an overcast day is obvious, but the light also changes according to the time of day and the season.

EVENING SUNLIGHT

COVE AT DUSK
by Rosalie Nadeau
The sun creates shadows, which present compositional possibilities. Evening light is often best, making shadows longer and colours richer. This wonderful impression of sunset colours uses mauve and yellow – complementary contrasts – to enhance the effect of the diagonal shadows leading to the dark verticals of the trees. To set the tonal key for the painting, the artist made the unusual choice of black paper, working up from the darkest to the lightest colours.

EARLY MORNING LIGHT

TWO WILLOWS by Patrick Cullen
At this time of day the light is at its gentlest. Tonal contrasts are slight and colours less vivid. By working in a high tonal key – that is, in predominantly pale colours – the artist conveys the cool luminosity of the early morning.

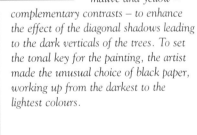

WATER

Pastels – either chalk or oil – are perfect for painting water. With chalk, the underlying colour of the water can be blended, with bright accents of more linear colour to define highlights and reflections on the surface. Oil pastels can be blended with turpentine for water-like movement.

CEDAR RIVER by L. C. Laird
Reflecting the cold evening light, the sluggish river breaks through the ice. Pale yellow and pink reflected light is scumbled over the textured paper and contrasted with blended greys and browns in the shadows.

A combination of shadows and reflections on still, ornamental ponds creates a challenge for the artist. The contrasts in this scene are stronger, but you will notice that the tonal range is wider with darker darks though the highlights are no brighter. A wide range of blues is necessary, too, for the more complicated composition, with greens for the foliage and weeds in the water.

For this African swamp with the sun breaking through the mist, the palette is warm with, amongst others, pale tints of ultramarine blue, yellow ochre, sap green and burnt sienna, contrasted with some darker accents in raw umber, grey-green and cool grey. Pale scumbles give the impression of the mist rising from the water. Note how the colours are taken through from one part of the painting to the other.

A stormy day blowing the tops off the waves is captured in a palette of blues of different tints with burnt umber, and some warm neutral greys for shadows and to give some contrast in temperature. The warm sandy colour of the support is also an important colour in the composition, showing through in all parts of the painting. Using fine grade sandpaper as a support allows the artist to build up the white water in areas of impasto.

SUNDOWN, RAMBHOLT by Margaret Glass
In the still evening, when the wind has died, a glorious sunset is reflected in the water in subtle shades of yellow and pink.

Moving Water

RYUZU FALLS, ABOVE LAKE CHUZENJI, NIKKO, JAPAN by Elsie Dinsmore Popkin
Working from dark to light, the artist scumbles blue shadows in the falls over the darks, and adds white highlights with short, sharp strokes.

PASTEL OVER GOUACHE

A dark, mottled gouache base is allowed to dry, and lively white pastel strokes are used to describe highlights in the white water.

1 *To create the effects of white water, first use a dark wash of not-too-dilute grey. Before it dries, take some absorbent paper twisted to a point and stipple this over the paint to give a mottled effect.*

185

2 *Once the paint is dry, take a white pastel stick and work it over the top. Keep the strokes descriptive of the rushing water by making short, lively strokes punctuated with stipples and points,*

created by twisting the stick on the paper.

3 *With a dark blue-grey mix, make further painted strokes over the pastel to increase the feeling of movement.*

A STUDY OF WHITE WATER by Doug Dawson
By focusing on a stretch of river, the artist creates a pattern of colours and tones that is semi abstract. Superimposed, broken strokes capture the drama of the rushing water.

ALAMEDA BEACH by Kitty Wallis
The quality of the evening light and the translucence of the aquamarine water work on the soul, providing food for thought.

OIL PASTELS AND TURPENTINE

Building a wave over an ultramarine-blue acrylic underpainting, the artist takes advantage both of the dry, almost waxy quality of oil pastels, and of their painterly dimension when blended with turpentine. This method of blending allows the colour to be moved around without flattening it in the later stages.

1 *Use broad pastel strokes, with the stick held on its side, over a dry acrylic underpainting, to describe the direction of the breaking wave and the distribution of tone.*

187

2 *Having worked up the impasto white crest, now dip your brush in turpentine and work into the pastel strokes to blend and add directional strokes, here reducing the overlaid white to a scumbled veil.*

3 *For flatter areas of blending, such as the reflective wall of rising water with the light shining through, use a finger to smear juicy colours together.*

OTHER TECHNIQUES

With soft pastels, the immediacy of crashing waves can be conveyed if the colours are applied freshly, without too much blending or superimposition of one colour on another. Try laying a watercolour wash first (on stretched watercolour paper), then break off pieces of pastel to use on their sides, making short strokes that interlock and sometimes overlap to indicate the fall of the light and the direction of the movement of the water. These strokes will contrast with the powerful explosion of spray from a crashing wave, which can be created in expressive, directional strokes of tinted whites and greys. For textured spray, stipple with the end of the chalk, twisting as you take the stick away. Anything is permissible if it works. You could try to create the texture of the spume by filing chalk onto a layer of adhesive gum arabic. You could also work on the finest grade of sandpaper, which will allow you to build up more layers of texture.

Oil pastels were made for rough seas. They can be mixed with turpentine for an expressive underpainting, which can be worked into with the dry sticks while it is still wet, and again when dry for a more chalky burst of spray.

Reflections

Reflections occur on moving water, but their effect is more generalized as the ruffled water breaks up the reflected image, making the colour less intense, and with only a suggestion of the form of the object reflected.

You will see only patches of colour if sky is reflected in moving water, while on flat parts of a river, the reflection will be clearer and more complete.

For a reflection to be good and clear, water needs to be flat and transparent so that, as soon as the surface is ruffled or the water is opaque, the reflections will be fragmented and blurred. As we have discovered, in any moving river you will find a wide variety of different states of water, all of which will reflect in different ways. With experience, you will learn about the relative reflectivity of these different states. Even after studying water for years, however, you are often

surprised. For instance, a moving river which appears flat does not always reflect as clearly as you might expect. You will find on closer inspection that this is because the surface is a simmering layer of water, which makes it opaque and distorted and does not reflect very well at all.

The fact that reflections are affected by the nature of the water means that you can use them to help describe the changing character of the surface, using repeated patches of reflected colour for gentle ripples, clearer reflections for areas of flatter water, and fragments of reflected colour in more agitated water.

RIVER ASH SERIES, SUMMER by John Plumb
Reflections distorted by movement in the water are expressed with pale, linear, snake-like marks over a dark base.

BUILDINGS

The spatial organization of individual buildings and architectural groups often provides a ready made composition, with the colours and textures of the various construction materials adding surface interest.

The colours and textures of pastels correspond well to features such as weathered brick, wood, stone and painted plasterwork. The medium's linear qualities also help to give definition to subjects composed of planes and angles.

A building often has a special character that makes it an attractive subject in itself. Its particular appeal can be stressed by the viewpoint that you take – distant or close, forward-facing or angled, with the building merging into or isolated from its surrounding context. The subject can also be enhanced by imaginative treatment of unusual effects of light and colour as well as basic physical attributes of shape, form and texture.

ROOFTOPS, SAN DONNINO by Patrick Cullen
As is often the case with old buildings, these seem to grow naturally out of the land, just as the trees do, and the artist treated them in the same way. He has given a good impression of place; the tiled roofs and thick walls are typical of the Italian countryside.

ROME FLATS
by Jane Strother

Cropping right into the uniform façades of the buildings so that neither the base nor the apex of the houses is seen creates a confrontational image softened by the warm, inviting colours. The artist's technique of combining oil paint and oil pastel to make the colour masses and loosely scrubbed textures perfectly complements the character of the image.

THE SMOKEHOUSE, CLEY by Margaret Glass

The awning in bright sunlight first drew the artist's interest, and was centrally placed in the composition. The warm colour of the sandpaper ground shows through the broken colour depicting stone and cobbles.

191

Towns and Cities

City districts also have their characteristic flavour, so pay attention to the predominant building material and the way in which the buildings are arranged.

Some towns have wide, straight streets with regimented rows of identical houses; in others, streets are narrow, and buildings vary. Create the feeling of urban bustle by including people, cars and typical 'street furniture', such as lamp-posts, railings, signs and benches.

Alternatively, you can depict a convincing townscape from a high viewpoint, such as an upstairs window. This allows you to see the entire layout of the place, and can provide an exciting composition, with rooftops forming patterns. If you live in a flat with a good view,

you are fortunate, and if not, there are often public buildings that provide suitable vistas.

If your subject is a single building, such as your own house, you will want to create a likeness, so make sure that the shape and proportions are accurate. But consider viewpoint and lighting as well, because they will affect your composition. It is not always wise to paint a building from directly in front; a three-quarter view conveys greater solidity as well as a more interesting look. Sunlight provides shadows that help to define the structures and give tonal contrast.

SUMMER EVENING, ST. MARTIN'S PLACE by Margaret Glass
You will usually want to include one or two figures in an urban scene, but people instantly attract the eye because we identify with them, so they can dominate the composition. The artist avoided this risk by treating the group of girls very broadly and setting up strong tonal contrasts on the building and statue behind, so that this area becomes the focal point.

ST. JOHN'S COLLEGE GATE, CAMBRIDGE
by Geoff Marsters
Although the building has little detail, its general proportions and the shapes of the windows are sufficient to communicate its style and identify it immediately to anyone familiar with the town. The artist's main theme is light and colour, and he conveyed the rich hues of a sunlit autumn day by using the same vivid palette for the trees and the building. This prevents the building from becoming too dominant.

If you choose a building as a subject, it is because you respond to it. You admire its proportions or the way it nestles into the landscape. An old building might attract you by the texture of its peeling paint or weathered wood. Try to identify the building's special features, and see if you can find ways of showing them off. A house set in an expanse of country, for example, would call for a distant view, expressing the interaction of man-made and natural features, or perhaps hinting at the isolated lives of the inhabitants.

Streets and Markets

Views of a town or village street are often interesting as a setting for human activity.

There is a fascinating contrast between the solid permanence of an architectural background and the colour and motion of people going about their business. The introduction of the figures enhances the sense of scale; the buildings may form a neutral backdrop to the human interest or may interact with and enclose them, depending on the viewpoint you take and the way you integrate different elements of the composition.

Street markets, colourful and containing a wealth of varied detail, are particularly fascinating subjects for drawing and painting. They exist in all areas of the world but are characteristically expressive of their own culture and community. They combine aspects of architectural, figure and still life composition and the vital interplay of moving and fixed forms.

MARKET STALL, PIAZZA BARTOLOMEO
by Diana Armfield
The cast shadow of the right-hand building gives this composition a predominantly cool cast, against which the sunlit corner of the far building stands out dramatically. Both architecture and figures are described with a subtle interplay of free linear marks that structure the forms and areas of shading and broken colour that give weight and solidity.

THE RED HOUSE
by Jane Strother

A streetscape atmosphere emerges from the close, acutely angled viewpoint in this composition, although its subject is a single building. The framing of the perspective suggests an unseen continuity. A combination of oil paint and pastel, vigorously rubbed and scribbled, is used to create the scrubbed textures of the colour-washed walls.

A FRENCH MARKET by Alan Oliver
By keeping detail to a minimum, the artist created a powerful impression of market bustle. The figures are sketched rather than drawn, with rapidly applied side strokes from a short length of pastel. The feeling of movement is continued into the background.

MEDITERRANEAN VILLAGE

The whitewashed houses, clear blue sky and deep shadows provide an attractive subject. The artist visited this village on a family holiday, and because time was limited, she developed the painting afterwards from a photograph. She departed from her visual reference in a number of ways, using the photograph to structure the composition and to help with details, but relying more on her memories of the colours and general atmosphere of the scene.

1 *After making a light charcoal drawing, the artist starts on the white buildings. The pastel is applied thickly here, and masking tape is used to keep the edges straight.*

3 *Because there is so much white in this painting, it was important to place the lightest tones first. With the white wall in place, it is easier to determine the colour for this shadow, created with strokes of red-brown over blue-grey.*

2 *The masking tape is removed, leaving a crisp edge. Notice that the pastel is not uniformly thick. To the left of the tape is an area where the paper shows through, suggesting the crumbling texture of the wall.*

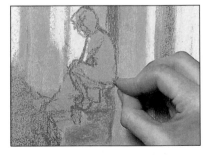

4 *The faint charcoal outline of the figure is strengthened with blue pastel ready to be filled with a mixture of this and other colours.*

5 *Small details are often left until the final stages of a painting, but this area of strong colour is important to the composition and colour scheme, so the artist establishes it before continuing with the walls.*

6 *Tones and colours are continually assessed. There was insufficient tonal contrast between the orange of the windows and the blue first laid down for the wall, so the blue is lightened with side strokes of white.*

7 *Shadows can easily dull through overblending. A variety of colours were laid over one another but were not blended, and the area is finally darkened and enriched with light side strokes of purple.*

8 *The figure is important but should not stand out too strongly, so it is treated almost as a silhouette; red-brown worked into the earlier blue-grey gives it a suggestion of form. The colours are similar to those of the shadows, which unifies the composition. The finished picture is above.*

197

ANIMALS AND BIRDS

The range of pastel techniques – linear strokes, broken colour, feathering, hatching and stippling – makes the medium ideal for representing animal textures.

Pastel is suited not only to the highly tactile qualities of fur and feathers, but also to the baggy, rough skins of animals such as the elephant and rhinoceros, and the smooth-haired hides of horses and cattle. As a dynamic colour medium, pastel readily accommodates bold markings such as spots and stripes, the vivid colour schemes of tropical birds, and the jewelled patterning of fish scales or snake skin.

WAYS AND MEANS

Because animals rarely pose, most artists find it difficult, at least at first, to draw from the living model. The obvious solution seems to be using photographs. This certainly widens the choice of creatures you can study at close quarters and avoids the problem of the animal walking away before you can put pastel to paper. However, a static photographic image can be lifeless and lacking in detail. When it is essential to work from photographs, be sure to allow your technique plenty of life of its own to convey your interest in the subject.

STUDY AND PRACTICE

Pets are the easiest live models to start with, or farm or zoo animals, depending on accessibility. When studying the real thing, you may find it helpful at first to spend at least as much time watching the animal as you do drawing it. Give yourself time to get used to the continual movement so that you can start to identify the animal's characteristic details of form and texture.

If you want to practice describing detail, you can work from stuffed museum exhibits. This enables you to study pattern and texture closely and unhurriedly, and to observe the ways a creature's markings relate to its physical structure. Anatomical studies are not essential to animal drawing, unless you want to take a scientific interest.

Bear in mind that the most detailed drawing of an animal is not necessarily the most realistic. When you look at a cat, a giraffe, or a bullfinch, you do not take in every hair, every colour patch, every barb on a feather. A drawing or painting is always as much about your own perception as it is about the sum total of your subject.

WINTER FEED
by Keith Bowen

This combination of animal and human subjects conveys very clearly the context of the image and the scale of the massive beasts. The composition is interestingly divided into solid blocks of colour by the strong vertical and horizontal stresses, but each colour area is carefully modelled tonally and given a distinctive texture built up with a dense network of individual pastel strokes. At 75 x 100 cm (30 x 40 in), the scale of the pastel rendering enables the artist to manipulate the linear textures very freely. It is worked on heavy white paper, which shows through in tiny glints among the dark tones of the animals' tough hides.

MAINE COON CAT by Stephen Paul Plant

The soft grey of the coloured ground provides a mid-tone from which to key in the brindled markings. The face and features are first drawn in detail, then the fur texture is developed. A little charcoal is applied as a base for the strong blacks and in finishing touches.

Sketches

When you are working from live models, quick sketches are an invaluable method of getting to know animal forms.

The free motion of a pastel stick enables you to respond very quickly to the movements of the subject, and you do not have the pressure to produce a highly finished image – a single continuous line sometimes catches the perfect impression of a graceful animal contour. Many sketches are just as satisfying in their own terms as are more lengthy and considered works.

Sketching sidesteps the problem of getting enough time to study the animal effectively, because your representations can be a series of rapid drawings according to what the animal is doing at any given time. Domestic and zoo animals develop routine movements and cycles of behaviour, so that you can count on an individual pose or movement recurring. With patience you will begin to recognize the elements that are essential to your representation, and develop effective ways of interpreting them in pastel.

ELEPHANT and COUGARS
by Stan Smith
In these two sketches the lines are loosely worked in oil pastel (part of the elephant's outline is in pencil), and the washed colour is laid in with oil paint thinned with turpentine. The rapid movements of the pastel strokes show how quickly the sketches were drawn, focusing on the contours and skin texture of the animals' bodies, and including only the most essential features.

Studies

A study is a much more detailed rendering than a sketch, typically requiring plenty of time for a rigorous visual analysis focusing on the exact form and texture of the animal.

A study is, in effect, a portrait, or likeness of the particular animal, whereas a sketch may be more freely concerned with the essential characteristics of the species and how these are displayed in typical poses and movements.

When working with pastel, you need to build the image patiently with gradual layering of many individual marks. You need time to do this, which almost certainly means that you will have to refer to photographs, as the animal will not maintain one pose for long. Ideally, you should combine live observation with photographic reference, so that your memory supplements the pictorial record. It is far preferable to take your own photos of a living creature than to work from pictures in books or magazines, and you can also use sketches as reference, taken from the model, a practice that enables you to relate your observations to the technical solutions that your medium can provide.

THE FIRST SUCKLE by Keith Bowen
The ewe's thick, rumpled wool is elaborated with light feathering strokes and curling linear marks, the massing of the pastel marks gradually building the forms. The body of the lamb is similarly modelled, controlling the weight of the strokes and the colour range to obtain the smoother texture and brighter tone of its fleece.

Environment

If you are going to represent an animal in the context of its usual environment, you need to consider the degree of detail you wish to achieve and the way your pastel techniques can construct an integrated image while appropriately describing separate aspects of the animal and its surroundings.

Because pastel is a versatile medium, you will find that the range of its marks and textures corresponds well to all kinds of background details – domestic interiors for studies of pets, landscape settings or man-made enclosures for farm and wild animals, sky or water for bird studies, and even the unusual underwater environment shown in the example below. But don't overlook the potential of mixed-media techniques – using

watercolours, for instance, to flood in large areas of land or sky, or drawing with graphite or coloured pencils to develop linear detail.

You can be as descriptive or impressionistic as you wish in representing the environment; a few brief marks can suggest the nature of the creature's habitat, but if you have drawn the animal in detail, you may prefer to apply the same precision to recording its surroundings.

HUMPBACK WHALE AND CALF by Stephen Paul Plant
When the subject is marine mammals or fish, the character of their environment is highly influential on the form and colouring of the creatures. Here the artist interprets both elements as a combination of blended colour gradations and fluid linear marks.

SHOW BULL by Keith Bowen

The arrangement of the composition places foremost attention on the massive bulk of the bull, the details of its stall and feed bucket helping to establish a sense of scale. The solid colour masses are built up with a dense network of overlaid shading and hatching.

DOE RABBIT AND HER KITTENS by Stephen Paul Plant

The technique of building texture with linear marks over flat colour is consistently applied to both the rabbits and their grassy background.

Birds

Birds are a wonderful subject for drawing and painting. They present a huge variety of form, size, texture and colour, from the compact bodies and discreet earthy colouring of ordinary garden species to the exuberant wings and crests and brilliant colours of tropical birds.

There is a stunning visual difference between a bird on the ground or perched on a branch and the same bird in flight with its wings fully extended.

Some artists specialize in bird studies and can spend all their working lives discovering the many variations on the theme. If you want to make this an area of special interest, you can gather references from a range of sources. First, and most important, you can observe and sketch birds in the wild. Details of form, colour and texture can be gleaned from photographs and

through museum studies of stuffed specimens. Exotic species can be seen live in enclosed avaries, and you can again supplement your knowledge of them with photographic references. There are many books describing the anatomical detail and flight mechanisms of birds, which can all add to your understanding of the subject.

If you make detailed studies of bird species and want to give your renderings a realistic context, don't forget to pay equal attention to correct information about their habitats.

BARN OWL by Stephen Paul Plant *The compact shape and formal detail of the owl in flight is emphasized by the loosely drawn dark background.*

FLAMINGOES by Kay Gallwey

The fluid areas of colour that establish the general shapes of the birds and the dark ground of the water surface were created by printing off a loosely worked oil painting onto paper. The oil colour was allowed to dry before the linear detail of the birds was freely drawn with bold pastel colours. Pastel strokes also describe the shimmering reflections of the flamingoes' colours on the water.

GREAT CRESTED GREBES by Stephen Paul Plant

There is an interesting contrast in the rounded shapes of the birds' bodies and the elongated forms of the crested heads with their long, pointed bills. The paper colour creates a unified tone that assists in the impression of the birds being partially camouflaged in their habitat.

DEMONSTRATION BY JUDY MARTIN

To draw an image, such as a cheetah, from life is obviously impossible. The photograph used as reference was a very dynamic shot, and the incomplete pose, with tail and foreleg cropped, was retained as appropriate to the sense of movement conveyed by the image. The artist had previously studied cheetahs through sketches made at the zoo.

1 *The artist is particularly interested in the camouflage patterns of the animals. The sandy colour of the paper forms the base colour both of the cheetah's fur and the dry, earthy background. The contours are freely sketched in yellow ochre.*

2 *Some of the cheetah's markings are drawn in black pastel to key in the darkest tones. Yellow, orange and brown tints in the fur are loosely indicated with rapid shading and broad, short side strokes.*

3 *The patches of light and shade surrounding the animal are blocked in, and further tones and colours are added to the fur, using gestural marks made with the pastel tip.*

4 *The artist begins to define the head, using the natural pattern of black lines around the eyes and nose, and the dark tufts behind the ears. With the stronger blacks in place, the colour detail is reworked more heavily.*

5 *The pattern of spots on the cheetah's body and ringed markings on the foreleg are thickly worked with the pastel tip. Around the black spots, the colour detail is developed by shading the linear marks, including the white fur highlighting the head and face.*

6 *The cast shadow under the body and tail is emphasized with a cold grey that contrasts with the warm yellows. The sunlight reflecting on the ground plane is similarly strengthened with the same pale yellow tint previously applied to the fur.*

7 *The final steps are to put finishing touches to the colour detail. Because the yellows now appear a little flat, stronger orange and red ochre patches are laid into the body and tail, and the spot pattern is reworked in black and sepia.*

CHEETAH
by Judy Martin

PORTRAIT AND FIGURE WORK

In the late 19th century, with the camera gaining popularity, there was alarm and despondence among artists and art lovers. How would portrait painters earn a living when the camera could produce perfect likenesses in a fraction of the time? 'Art is dead,' people said. But it was not.

Painted portraits have continued to coexist with photographs, and artists still find the human face and figure among the most exciting and challenging of subjects.

And challenging they are, because in this branch of painting you cannot get away with poor drawing and inaccurate observation. Errors such as wrongly proportioned bodies are immediately noticeable because the subject is so familiar.

HUMAN PROPORTIONS

Accuracy in drawing and painting is mainly a matter of practice – of training yourself to see your subject in an analytical way. But it does help to have a few guidelines to fall back on, so that if your picture looks wrong you can work out why. Human faces and bodies vary widely – that is what makes them so interesting – but there are some basic rules about human proportions.

The body is about seven and a half heads high. (The head is used by artists as the unit of measurement.) If a person is standing with arms hanging free, the fingertips reach to about mid-thigh, and the body's halfway point is at the crotch.

A typical error is to make hands and feet too small; nearly all beginners do this. Feet have to support the entire weight of the body, so they need to be relatively large. The length of the foot is about the same as the height of the head. Hands are working tools that need strength. An outstretched hand will cover the face.

There are standard proportions for faces also. The bottom of the eye sockets is the midpoint of the head, and the eyes are about one eye's distance from each other.

SETTING THE POSE

Some portraits focus on the head, with the body cropped off just below the base of the neck. These are known as head-and-shoulders. A half-length portrait includes the top part of the body and the hands, while a full-length is the entire figure, seated or standing.

Whichever category you choose, do not rush into the painting

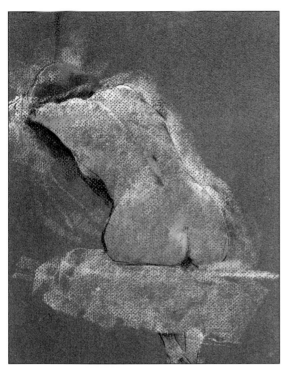

A LIFE STUDY by
Clifford Hatts

without giving serious consideration to the way you pose the sitter. Aim for a natural, relaxed look, even in a head-and-shoulders portrait, where you will not see much of the body. If you decide on a half- or full-length, find a chair or sofa in which the sitter both looks and feels at ease. Bear in mind that posing for a portrait is tiring, so ask your subject's advice on the most comfortable position. You will often find that this contributes to the likeness, since people have characteristic postures that they assume naturally, whether seated or reclining.

You might even choose an outdoor setting, which creates a more natural and spontaneous impression. This would be suitable for a painting of a child, for example, or an avid gardener – resting in a deck chair surrounded by his or her horticultural creations.

Clothes, too, can help convey a feeling of the person, so it is not usually good to dress your sitters in their Sunday best, but rather have them wear their everyday attire. You can take this idea further and include in the painting some objects that hint at the sitter's interests. This is a device often used by portrait painters: An artist is shown holding paintbrushes, or a writer has a pile of books on a table nearby.

Standing Figures

The standing figure is a dynamic form, the body seen in full proportion and with the tension of imminent movement – since few people stand stock still for long.

Every standing pose has its own specifics of weight and balance, for instance, the torso may be firmly supported on both legs, or the weight may be shifted to one side with one leg bent or extended. Other factors that contribute to the balance of the pose are the angle of the head in relation to the body, and the disposition of the arms.

The individual character of the figure in a particular pose is a combination of internal and external detail. The simple outline of a figure can be very telling, but the volumes of which it is composed, and their formal relationships, create the solid sense of realism.

Clothing adds colour to your rendering and is also expressive of both form and character. It makes useful surface detail, but look for the ways in which it can also describe aspects of the pose, emphasizing or concealing the contours of the body and adding to the rhythms and tensions of the figure.

A NORFOLK BEACH by Alan Oliver

None of these figures is treated in detail, and the more distant ones are just decisive flicks of pastel. They carry perfect conviction, however, because the artist has observed the shapes of their postures so well. The figure bending over the buggy, for example, is suggested with a few diagonal lines. Bold, lively pastel marks bring a strong sense of movement.

PEANUTS HUCKO
by Carole Katchen

Although the body shapes are not precisely realistic, they are wonderfully expressive of the musicians' energy and tension, the active qualities of each pose enhanced by the loose hatching of the pastel strokes.

SYLVIE AT THE PARIS RENDEZVOUS
by Irene Wise

Vigorous gestural drawing creates a bold image capturing the mood and character of the subject. The contours of the figure are simply expressed but are finely descriptive of the body's weight and balance.

Movement

Very rapid motion is difficult to convey, although as previous examples have demonstrated, precise rendering of a split-second action can be highly descriptive, seeming to encompass the essential character of the action.

A very different approach is taken here, using the calligraphic qualities of the medium and the free motions of the hand to travel along with the whole movement, building up a dense network of related marks and overlapping contours. This is particularly effective with stylized or repeated movements, such as dancing or exercising, as certain visual clues and points of reference return throughout the cycle.

This needs a vigorous, uninhabited technique – the drawing should emerge quite freely. There is always an element of experiment, and some sketches will be more successful than others, but because you will be working rapidly, you should soon achieve some interesting results.

**T'AI CHI EXERCISE
by George Cayford**
When describing the continual motion of a figure, it is necessary to guide the pastel freely in direct response to the movements as they are seen. Speed is essential, thus the pastel is used here mainly as a line medium, with varying colours explaining different sequences of the exercise.

FISHING, BANYAN LAKE by Kitty Wallis
The artist was prompted by the relationship between the movement of the bodies and that of the water, and expressed this rhythmic flow through her pastel marks. The strokes on the figures follow the direction of their movement, emphasizing the diagonal thrust, while inventively varied marks suggest the shifting of the water.

FIGURES IN ACTION

Whether engaged in sports or performing everyday tasks, people in action make an exciting painting subject, but a challenging one. Especially if you work from photographs, remember to use the technique that gives an impression of movement: Strong linear strokes or scribbled marks are better than soft blends. And back up photographic reference with information; become familiar with the way the body behaves when it is in motion by observing people and making quick sketches whenever you can.

213

Groups

Figure groups can represent all of the visual points of interest of the single figure, but their interactions are the keynote of the image.

The elements of composition are as important as the details of individual form and character – alignment of the figures, the relationships of size and proportion, the space or closeness between them, and the relative distance from the viewer.

The grouping may be random, as with people on the street, or it may be due to a common purpose – of people coming together to share an activity or form an audience. The active and passive relationships between the figures can be expressed in the composition, whether or not the group's full context and surroundings are portrayed.

JAZZ AT THE MUSEUM by Carole Katchen
The consistency of style and technique in this composition is employed in emphasizing variations of form and character in the informal figure group. Individual body shapes and poses are broadly conveyed but incorporate many subtle nuances of form and direction. The controlled colour scheme effectively suggests a particular quality of interior light.

Children

The most common problem in drawing children is identifying the precise characteristics that make them childlike – they are not mini-versions of adult people.

A child's head is larger in proportion to the body than is the adult's; the limbs are mobile and flexible, but the chubbiness typical of young children disguises bone and muscle structure.

Another difficulty is getting a child to pose. If you are working from life, you need to choose a style and technique that enable you to work quickly or can accommodate changes in the pose if the child becomes fidgety. If you are working on a more complex composition that needs prolonged attention to detail, you may need to work from photographic reference and, if possible, ask the child to pose briefly to check any elements of form and posture that are not clear from your reference pictures.

CURIOSITY by Barry Freeman

Children have an easy suppleness that enables them unconsciously to create graceful poses in the course of ordinary action and play. In this composition, the two bodies are linked in a rhythmic, self-contained shape at the centre of the composition, the more striking because detail of their surroundings is minimized. The natural colour range and gentle technique express the simple pleasure of the subject.

215

Portraits

Portraiture is one of the classic themes of pastel painting, very richly expressed in the work of 18th-century artists such as Rosalba Carriera (1674–1757), Maurice Quentin de la Tour (1704–1788) and Jean-Baptiste Perroneau (1715–1783).

It was carried through into the modern age by artists as diverse as Henri de Toulouse-Lautrec (1864–1901) and Umberto Boccioni (1882–1916). Whereas the earlier artists took advantage of the smooth blending qualities and subtle tints of soft pastels to produce detailed, complex portrayals of facial features and lavishly styled accessories, their modern counterparts preferred to exploit the medium's expressive qualities of brilliant colour and linear vitality.

THE LIKENESS

Portraits take many forms and involve different degrees of visual analysis, but their essence lies in creating a likeness. This does not necessarily mean accurate copying of a person's features; sometimes the detail of the features is indistinct, or even absent, but the character of that person emerges vividly from minimal visual cues.

The best portraits contain something about the mood and style of the sitter. It may pay for you to risk slight exaggeration of the most dominant features, to emphasize the person's clothing, to pose them in a way that demonstrates an unusual but characteristic gesture. You can also select clothing, props and background that give the subject a particular context and provide you with additional formal elements of composition that you can work with inventively.

ERICK by Sally Stride
This is a charming character study, although details of the facial features are deliberately vague. The shapes of head, body and limbs and the overall posture are highly descriptive.

Heads

The face is usually the focal area of a portrait, so it is common that pastel portraits concentrate on the head. This single aspect of the person presents many challenges to the artist. The shapes of individual features are crucial, as are the colours of the skin tones and the way the hair frames the face.

Facial features – eyes, noses and mouths – are difficult to draw. While some artists have the ability to catch the precise shape and form with a few brief marks, others find these details extremely troublesome and fail to marry observation and technique. You need to study carefully the precise shapes and apparent outlines of the features, the way they are modelled with subtle shifts of light and shadow, the tiny colour changes that give life to eyes and mouths.

AGE AND CONCERN
The age of the model is a fascinating aspect of portraiture because different stages of life are repre-sented by different kinds of visual information. The most obvious is skin texture. Young skin is typically smooth with fresh colouring; ageing brings character lines and wrinkles, stronger shadowing of the features, and skin tones that are weathered or faded.

Other important cues are contained in the structure of the face, the shape of the head, and the posture of the sitter. In children's

faces the features occupy a relatively small proportion of the whole head, and details are unformed. In adulthood the underlying structure of bone and muscle shapes the face, and individual features become strongly defined – a heavy jawline or prominent nose, for instance. With age the patterns shift again, eyes and mouth perhaps becoming sunken, skin more heavily folded, and the hairline receding, thus altering the proportions of face and head.

THE CURCUIT JUDGE
by Urinia Christy Tarbet

ARRANGING THE POSE

The artist has chosen to create colour interest by swathing the sitter in a patterned shawl and posing her against the backdrop of a decorative curtain. This gives a very rich surrounding that enhances the dramatic contrast of the pale skin tones and dark hair. The artist's easel is set up at an angle that enables her to see both the sitter and the drawing at the same time so that her observations are quickly and directly transferred to the paper.

1 *The general shapes of head, hair, face and upper body are loosely blocked in with bold linear marks and hatching. In places, the pastel is spread by the movement of the artist's hand and by deliberate rubbing with the fingers. This initial, sketchy stage creates a general impression of the local colours in each element of the portrait. The darker pastel colours are used to define the basic structure of the head. From the increasingly dense network of coloured lines, the modelling of face and hair emerges more clearly. The eyes are already quite sharply defined, as these are always a focal point in a portrait.*

2 *The range of tones and colours is extended overall, in some places boldly stated and in others subtly blended by finger rubbing*

3 *The whole surface is kept active at every stage. Although the use of colour is now more elaborate, the rendering remains open and workable due to the loose weaving of strokes.*

4 *The modelling of the face and variation of the flesh tints is developed more intensely. Luminous highlighting is applied to the eyes and the projecting curves of the face.*

5 *Strong directional lines describe the flowing hair, the colours providing greater contrast of tone. A similar treatment is applied to the folds of the patterned shawl.*

6 *Having added mid-toned greys and mauves to the shadowing around the eye sockets and nose, the artist adds crisp finishing touches that bring back the focus and clarity of the eyes.*

PORTRAIT OF STEFANIE
by Kay Gallwey

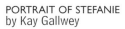

Glossary

Blending Fusing colours together, with the fingers, a rag or a torchon.

Blocking in Establishing the main forms and composition of a picture with areas of colour and tone.

Complementary Colours Those colours that are opposite each other on the colour wheel, such as red and green, yellow and violet, blue and orange. Each one increases the intensity of the other when they are juxtaposed.

Crosshatching A technique of criss-crossing lines of colour to create a fine mesh of colour and tone.

Feathering The technique of making light, diagonal strokes over another colour to lighten, darken, or otherwise modify it.

Fixing Spraying a substance onto a pastel so that the colour does not smudge or drop off the paper. Fixatives are varnishes applied with a sprayer, mouth blower, or atomizer.

Hatching A technique of creating areas of tone or colour with fine, parallel strokes following one direction.

Hue The term used for a pure colour found on a scale ranging through the spectrum – that is, red, orange, yellow, green, blue, indigo and violet.

Impasto A technique of applying pastel or paint thickly so that none of the support shows through.

Optical mixing The juxtaposition of blobs of colours so that the pigments do not actually mix, but at a certain distance appear to do so.

Overhand strokes Strokes applied with a pencil or pastel stick held between the thumb and forefinger. Holding the implement this way allows the artist to exercise the greatest control and accuracy over the marks made.

Pointillism A method of applying colour in a series of dots rather than with strokes or in flat areas.

Scumbling Applying colour loosely over another colour to give an irregular, broken surface.

Secondary colours The three colours formed by mixing pairs of primary colours: orange (red and yellow), green (yellow and blue) and violet (red and blue).

Sgraffito A technique of a incising into pastel or paint to create texture. Any type of mark can be created using any sharp instrument, from a pin to your fingernail.

Stippling Applying colour by using little dots of colour rather than flat areas or strokes.

Support The term applied to the material which provides the surface on which a painting or drawing is executed, for example, canvas, board or paper.

Temperature The term used to describe the relative warmth or coolness of a colour. For instance, orange and red are warmer than blue and green.

Tertiary colours Any colour formed by mixing a primary with a secondary colour.

Tone In painting and drawing, tone is the measure of light and dark on a scale of gradations between black and white. Every colour has an inherent tone; for example, yellow is light while Prussian blue is dark. But a coloured object or surface is also modified by the light falling on it, and an assessment of the variation in tonal values may be crucial to the artist's ability to indicate the three-dimensional form of an object.

Toothy A degree of texture or coarseness in a surface which allows painting or drawing material to adhere to the support.

Torchon (or tortillon) A stump of rolled paper used to blend colours.

Underhand strokes Strokes made with a pencil or pastel stick held in the palm of the hand and controlled by the thumb and fingers. The strokes produced are broad and sketchy and useful for covering large areas.

Index

Picture Credits

The material in this book previously appeared in:

Pastel School; Light - How to See It, How To Paint It; Master Strokes Pastel; Pastel Painting Techniques; How To Draw And Paint; The Encyclopedia Of Pastel Techniques; Colour - How To See It, How To Paint It; Tonal Values - How To See Them, How To Paint Them; Painting Shapes & Edges; The Encyclopedia Of Flower Painting Techniques; The Illustrated Book Of Painting Techniques; Water - How To see It, How To Paint It; Light - How To See it, How To Paint It.